D0328814

METAPHYSICAL
TO AUGUSTAN

METAPHYSICAL TO AUGUSTAN

Studies in Tone and Sensibility in the Seventeenth Century

GEOFFREY WALTON
Senior Lecturer in English in the University College of the Gold Coast

BOWES & BOWES

First published in 1955 by
Bowes & Bowes Publishers Limited
3 Henrietta Street
London W.C.2

Printed by Balding & Mansell, London and Wisbech

TO THE MEMORY
OF MY MOTHER

PREFACE

THE CHAPTERS that make up this book have grown out of the study I made before the war, as a Research Scholar of Downing College, Cambridge, of Cowley and his representative significance in mid-seventeenth-century literary history. Although twelve years have separated the first drafting of this part of the book from the completion of the whole, I think that certain consistent themes run through it and that one of the patterns discernible in seventeenth-century poetry emerges. This pattern may be described as the evolution of wit, especially as it manifests itself in the social tone of the poets, from the age of Donne to that of Dryden and the Augustans. I am particularly concerned with the transition, of which Cowley is the great example. I have not, however, thought it necessary to write a separate chapter on Waller and Denham and the beginnings of Neo-Classicism. This is well-explored territory, and I have preferred to keep to the less-known marches and show routes which lead in from the Metaphysicals. I feel that the Neo-Classic reaction against the Metaphysicals has received, as a reaction, plenty of attention from Johnson onwards; a recent American study, *Donne to Dryden: the Revolt against the Metaphysicals*, by R. L. Sharpe, exemplifies the traditional point of view. He amasses much interesting material but, I am sure, misinterprets it. I have tried to indicate that a more gradual and less straightforward development took place. Dryden did not merely reject the conceit; he adapted and used it.

This book is offered as an essay in literary criticism, an attempt to describe as objectively as possible what a group of seventeenth-century poets mean, separately and as a group, to one twentieth-century reader. For such a study historical knowledge of many kinds is essential both for explanation and as a negative check — to prevent one attributing to the poet meanings and ideas which could not possibly be in his work — but though I think that the appreciation of the spirit of seventeenth-century civilization in its many phases is an important part of the experience of reading its literature, I am sure that it is not possible, and pointless if it were, to read and judge as if one were a contemporary. One is grateful for much information to Professor Tuve and other recent literary scholars, but they leave us with the fundamental problem of how to read the poems. Whatever their similarity in principles of rhetoric and construction, the seventeenth-century poets are not usually like the sixteenth-century ones, and differ from and resemble each other in ways they themselves probably never dreamt of. Bearing all relevant historical information in mind, one still has the task of analysing the poems as they affect oneself and arriving at a judgement of value.

In making constant references to the social setting of literature and also to its wider intellectual affiliations, I have rested heavily on the appropriate work of others. I hope that I have made all the necessary acknowledgements in footnotes, and I think that I can claim that, where I have made assertions of a social nature, there is other historical evidence to support that of the poetry itself, which, though the product of the sensibilities of living men and women, may perhaps be impugned as more concerned with the ideal than the actual.

I have, I think, made my critical debts clear in the body of the text and in footnotes. I should also like especially to thank Professor G. Bullough and Professor V. da Sola Pinto, who recently read through the MS. and made valuable suggestions. For his constant interest and encouragement during many years I must express a more than ordinary gratitude to Dr F. R. Leavis, to whom, as my original supervisor in English studies, I feel that it would be neither fulsome nor pretentious to say in the words of the subject of my second chapter:

I owe
All that I am in arts, all that I know.

GEOFFREY WALTON

ACKNOWLEDGEMENTS

CHAPTERS 3 and 6 of this book have appeared in shorter versions in *Scrutiny* and *Politics and Letters* respectively; our acknowledgements are due to the editors.

CONTENTS

I

SEVENTEENTH-CENTURY IDEAS OF WIT: AN INTRODUCTORY CHAPTER

ONE IS CONSCIOUS of a greater homogeneity in early seventeenth-century poetry than in the poetry of any other age except the Augustan and the word 'wit' has been generally accepted as an inclusive designation. Except with the very limited connotations with which we are familiar in everyday usage, the word went out of circulation as a critical term after the eighteenth century, when it was, in fact, so taken for granted that even Johnson thought it unnecessary to define it when writing at length on the subject in his *Life of Cowley*. His critical study opens:

> The ode on wit is almost without rival. It was about the time of Cowley that *Wit*, which had till then been used for Intellection, in contradistinction to *Will*, took the meaning whatever it be, which it now [1779] bears.

Johnson is quite inadequate here, of course, but it is pretty clear that in the seventeenth century wit had a special and individual meaning. As a general description the suggestions put forward by Mr Eliot in the essay on Marvell have not really been surpassed:

> We are baffled in the attempt to translate the quality indicated by the dim and antiquated term wit into the equally unsatisfactory nomenclature of our own time. . . . It is confused with erudition because it belongs to an educated mind, rich in generations of experience; and it is confused with cynicism because it implies a constant inspection and criticism of experience. It involves, probably, a recognition, implicit in the expression of every experience, of other kinds of experience which are possible. . . .

I want to re-examine what seventeenth-century poets and critics themselves said about wit and see whether one can find there any accounts which give us further help in interpreting the poetry to ourselves as distinct from merely illustrating the historical context, whether one can find any explicit realization of what wit was as a basic quality of the poetry and of how it evolved from the age of Donne to that of the Augustans.

For this purpose Cowley's *Ode. Of Wit* provides a valuable focus. Standing as he does, a transitional figure between the Metaphysical and Cavalier Schools and Dryden and the Augustans, Cowley is a key figure and the ode shows us, explicitly and by implication, a great many of the qualities of his poetry which I shall later expatiate on in detail. That Johnson singled out Cowley as the most representative and the best Metaphysical poet, and furthermore found in him something which seemed so familiar that he felt he did not need to try to define it, is significant and important. The spirit of his poetry was peculiarly congenial to the eighteenth century and much of his work is, in fact, an early example of the Augustan mode. To put the matter briefly as a preliminary to discussion, Metaphysical and early seventeenth-century wit in a wider sense might be defined as a spiritual and intellectual poise, Restoration wit as a social poise. In Cowley one finds wit of both kinds very clearly visible, as his poetry easily yields up its full effect. It is, as a matter of fact, difficult to find early seventeenth-century statements on the nature of wit which are more than formal rhetorical or grammatical gestures. Ben Jonson gives no general account beyond a quotation from Aristotle on the madness of the poet and a reference to 'divine instinct'; elsewhere he keeps to matters of detail. It is, however, necessary to qualify my generalization about wit in his case more than in any other. Combined with his intellectual discipline and precision, he has in his non-dramatic verse a uniquely polite and civilized social tone and seems inspired by the very spirit of urbanity. In fact Jonson was not only Donne's greatest contemporary lyric poet and joint progenitor with him of the Cavaliers but also the creator of a manner in poetry which outlasted his immediate influence; it can even be said to have by-passed Dryden and to have found its greatest exponent in Pope. One finds the characteristic Metaphysical wit both manifested and described in Carew's remarkable Elegy on Donne, which implies a conception covering the whole creative process when he writes:

Since to the awe of thy imperious wit
Our stubborne language bends, made only fit
With her tough-thick-rib'd hoopes to gird about
Thy Giant phansie, which had prov'd too stout
For their soft melting Phrases.

This explosive idea is echoed — whether by a coincidence or not — in the following passage from Davenant's Preface to *Gondibert*, which is, I think, another valuable illustration from the earlier half, of the century:

> *Wit* is not only the luck and labour, but also the dexterity of thought rounding the world like the Sun, with unimaginable motion, and bringing swiftly home to the memory universall surveys. It is the Souls Powder, which when suppress . . . blows up the restraint . . . and breaks through all about it (as far as the utmost it can reach), removes, uncovers, makes way for light, where darkness was inclosed, till great bodies are more examinable by being scattered into parcels; till all that find its strength . . . worship it for its effects as derived from the Deity. It is in Divines, Humility, Exemplariness and Moderation, in Statesmen, Gravity, Vigilance, Benigne Complacency, Secrecy, Patience and Dispatch: in leaders of Armies, Valor, Painfullness, Temperance, Bounty, Dexterity in punishing and rewarding, and sacred Certitude of Promise. It is in Poets a full comprehension of all recited in all these, and an ability to bring those comprehensions into action, when they shall so far forget the true measure of what is of greatest consequence to humanity (which are things righteous, pleasant and useful), as to think the delights of greatness equall to that of Poesy; or the Chiefs of any Profession more necessary to the world, than excellent Poets.[1]

Davenant was not a distinguished thinker and is here inclined to flounder among words, but he undoubtedly wishes to convey a conception of wit which includes all the powers of the imagination and of poetic creation. The first part of his account resembles in general purport the well-known definitions of Hobbes and Dryden:

> Time and Education beget Experience: Experience begets Memory; Memory begets Judgement and Fancy; Judgement begets the strength and structure, and Fancy begets the ornaments of a Poem. . . .[2]

1 See *Critical Essays of the Seventeenth Century*, ed. Spingarn, vol. II, p. 21. *Gondibert* itself, one must emphasize, is decidedly not a product of the kind of imaginative process described in the preface, but of something much more superficial. Cowley, writing in a very Neo-Classic mood, praised it as an example of reformed 'heroick poesy'.

2 *Answer to Davenant*, in Spingarn, *op. cit.*, p. 59.

> Wit in the poet, or *Wit Writing* . . . is no other than the faculty of imagination in the writer, which like a nimble spaniel, beats over and ranges through the field of the memory, till it springs the quarry it desires to represent. *Wit Written* is that which is well defined, the happy result of thought or product of the imagination. . . . So the first happiness of the poet's imagination is properly invention, or finding of the thought, the second is fancy, or the variation, deriving and moulding, of that thought, as the judgement represents it proper to the subject; the third is elocution, or the art of clothing and adorning that thought, so found and varied, in apt, significant, and sounding words. . . .[3]

But Davenant keeps an idea of afflatus which they carefully secularize, and the Ptolemaic sun had after all a greater range than the nimblest spaniel — Davenant had himself rounded the world in imagination to seek images to offer *To the Lady Olivia Porter. Upon New Year's Day*.[4] 'Scattering into parcels' suggests the abundant and surprising products of the 'Giant phansie' which passion so often inspired in the early seventeenth century, as well as entertaining displays of verbal pyrotechnics. His last sentence offsets the idea of sorting out 'fixities and definites' for future collection by a suggestion of unification and synthesis. The 'full comprehension' claimed for the poet seems to imply that he 'brings the whole soul of man into activity, with the subordination of its faculties to each

3 Preface to *Annus Mirabilis*, *Essays*, ed. Ker, vol. I, p. 14.

4 His poem is worth attention both for its skilful arrangement of rich and far-fetched images and for its ironic astringency:

> Goe! hunt the whiter Ermine! and present
> His wealthy skin, as this dayes Tribute sent
> To my *Endimion's* Love; Though she he farre
> More gently smooth, more soft than Ermines are!
> Goe! climbe that Rock! and when thou there hast found
> A Star, contracted in a Diamond,
> Give it *Endimion's* Love, whose glorious Eyes
> Darken the starry Jewels of the Skies!
> Goe! dive into the Southern Sea! and when
> Th'ast found (to trouble the nice sight of Men)
> A swelling Pearle: and such whose single worth,
> Boasts all the wonder which the Seas bring forth;
> Give it *Endimion's* Love! whose ev'ry Teare
> Would more enrich the skilful Jeweller.
> How I command! how slowly they obey!
> The churlish *Tartar*, will not hunt to-day:
> Nor will that lazy, sallow *Indian* strive
> To climbe the Rock, nor that dull *Negro* dive.
> Thus Poets like to Kings (by trust deceiv'd)
> Give oftner what is heard of, than receiv'd.

other according to their relative worth and dignity'. This large description of wit must be supplemented by a sort of secondary description of it as the play of the critical intelligence over the emotional content of the poem — Johnson's 'intellection', which is one's more usual impression of the quality.

Dryden and Restoration critics also use wit to mean the whole process of writing poetry, but they had a very different conception of that process as a result of the scientific movement, of Neo-Classic theories and of the changes in social life. A further quotation from Hobbes will show how closely the change in the attitude to poetry was bound up with the changes in the nature of society:

> That which giveth a Poem the true and natural Colour consisteth in two things; which are *To know well*, that is to have the images of nature in the memory distinct and clear; and *To know much*. A sign of the first is perspicuity, propriety, and decency. . . .
>
> From *Knowing much* proceedeth the admirable variety and novelty of Metaphors and Similitudes. . . . And the want thereof compelleth a Writer to expressions that are either defac'd by time, or sullied with vulgar and long use.[5]

A certain fullness of life was being deliberately forced out of English poetry in the name of the social and scientific virtues of correctness and decorum. Paradoxically, there was a decided coarsening of feeling.

The official attitude of the Royal Society towards 'the delightful Deceit of Fables' is well known. Dryden's descriptions of wit and imagination represent a more moderate position, and the degree of scientific reasonableness and clarity that he favours corresponds very fairly to the actual extent of that influence on verse. Imaginative writing could not be further modified without changing into something else. The influence of the new science blends with those of Neo-Classicism and the new social code in varied combinations. Reason, Truth and Nature were obviously watchwords of all three worlds, and natural philosophers and men of letters met together in Park and coffee-house, where the conversation provided the idiom of Restoration writing. Cowley himself, as Sprat tells us,

5 *Answer to Davenant*, *Critical Essays of the Seventeenth Century*, ed. Spingarn, vol. II., p. 63. Hobbes later went further and equated wit and judgement: 'Where Wit is wanting, it is not Fancy that is wanting, but Discretion. Judgement therefore without Fancy is Wit, but Fancy without Judgement is not' (*Leviathan*, ed. Waller, p. 44).

'forsook the Conversation, but never the Language of the City and the Court'. In a polite and scientific world immediate intelligibility, even in recitation, also became a criterion of value for poetry, and hence Cowley can write:

> Persius (who, you use to say, you do not know whether he be a good Poet or no, because you cannot understand him, and who therefore (I say) I know to be not a good poet).[6]

One remembers, in contrast, that Ben Jonson wrote in praise of Donne:

> Longer a knowing, than most wits do live.

The urbanity of that day had been the subtler and more intimate spirit of a more select world in which 'rare poems [asked] rare friends'. Sir Thomas Pope Blount collects together in his *De Re Poetica* (1694) the most authoritative statements of Neo-Classic principles; here Dryden's remarks are considerably expanded and the poet is told how to make his work at once 'apt, clear, natural, splendid, and numerous'. A polite man-of-the-worldly tone is implied in Blount's first quotation on the mood for poetic composition which comes from Cowley's preface of 1656:

> The truth is, for a man to write well, it is necessary to be in a good humour.

The social denotation of wit, especially in its secondary meaning, is very apparent when Dryden equates dramatic wit with the conversation of gentlemen; 'the coolness and discretion which is necessary to a poet'[7] amounts to a kind of tact.

Whether one uses the term wit, or imagination, or fancy, one can say, I think, using rather portentous phrases, that the spirit of early seventeenth-century poetry tended to be at once centrifugal and inclusive, that of later seventeenth-century and Augustan poetry centripetal and exclusive. The poets of both ages used their minds in writing, but those of the former used them rather to expand, of the latter rather to limit their poetry.

It seems to me that Cowley's *Of Wit* stands between my

6 Essay on *The Dangers of Procrastination*, *Essays, Plays and Sundry Verses*, ed. Waller, p. 454.

7 *The Dramatic Poetry of the last Age*, *Essays*, ed. Ker, vol. I, pp. 171-7, and *Author's Apology for Heroic Poetry and Poetic Licence*, *ibid.*, pp. 186 and 190.

Sir Richard Blackmore's *Essay Upon Wit* gives the definition: 'Wit is a Qualification of Mind, that raises and enlivens cold Sentiments and plain Propositions, by giving them an elegant and surprising turn', which suggests the art of the conversationalist.

quotations from Davenant and Hobbes, both as to critical theory and poetic practice, and it is the more interesting in that they were certainly in frequent contact with him in the English exiled colony in Paris where he probably wrote the ode. Dr Leavis says that here Cowley 'expounds and discusses wit in a manner and spirit quite out of resonance with the Metaphysical mode — quite alien and uncongenial to it, with a reasonableness that has little to do with the "tough reasonableness" underlying Marvell's lyric grace (a grace of which Cowley has nothing). It is a spirit of good sense, of common sense, appealing to the criterion that the coming age will refine into "Reason, Truth and Nature".'[8] This suggests the kind of border line that Cowley occupies and the kind of decline of the Metaphysical school that he represents. The opening repetition: 'Tell me, oh tell . . .' is typical of him and looks forward to one of his besetting faults, his tendency to simulate inspiration, 'florid talk' which he himself condemned:

> Such were the *Numbers* which could call
> The *Stones* into the *Theban* wall.

Dr Leavis suggests a curious 'instability' between this bardic note and the tentative definitions of stanzas 8 and 9. The fact that the ode defines mainly by negatives is, I think, significant. It suggests an idea of social correctness; Cowley rules out the things that are not done — 'Rather than *all things Wit* let none be there'[9] and:

> Much less can that have any place
> At which a *Virgin* hides her face.

When we gather up the positives we find again a state of uncertainty:

> Yonder we saw it plain; and here 'tis now,
> Like *Spirits* in *a Place*, we know not *How*.

> All ev'ry where, like Mans, must be the *Soul*,
> And *Reason*, the *Inferior Powers* controul!

> What is it then, which like the *Power Divine*
> We only can by *Negatives* define?

> In a true piece of *Wit* all things must be,
> Yet all thing there *agree*.

8 *Revaluation*, p. 30.
9 When Dryden quotes this in the Preface to *An Evening's Love* (*loc. cit.*, vol. I) the context has a strongly social reference.

As in the *Ark*, joyn'd without force and strife,
All *Creatures* dwelt; all *Creatures* that had *Life*.
Or as the *Primitive Forms* of all
(If we compare great things with small)
Which without *Discord* or *Confusion* lie
In that strange *Mirror* of the *Deitie*.

The key words, on the one hand 'like *Spirits* in a *Place*' and 'like the *Power Divine*', on the other '*Reason*', '*agree*' and 'without *Discord* or *Confusion*', belong to different conceptions of the imagination. The idea of a mysterious force sorts with Davenant's description, while that of an organizing reason seems nearer to Hobbes and Dryden. Cowley effects a kind of reconciliation in the figure of the mirror, but he turns away in the last stanza to concrete examples which he can recognize:

I'll only shew your *Lines*, and say, *'Tis this*,

and one has a final impression of honest hesitancy between two theories, much as one feels that Cowley never found any one style of writing completely congenial.

In my later chapters on Cowley I endeavour to show how wit displays itself, and to some extent develops in character with the changing character of the times. A comparison between his tone and that of Marvell comes naturally, and appropriately, towards the end. Marvell, except for a few borrowings from Cowley and his admiration for Rochester's satires,[10] stands apart from his age as a poet as he did in later life as a man. He gives us a perfect fusion of the wit of Donne and the wit of Jonson; his urbanity far surpasses Dryden's and, as has already been suggested, one is tempted to see a poetic strain running through him from Jonson to Pope.[11] It is unfortunate that he left so few overt critical statements, as *The Garden* shows that he had profound ideas on the creative powers of the mind. A group of late and decidedly minor Metaphysicals gather naturally round Cowley as exemplifying similar poetic features.

My last contemporary quotation on wit dates from the year before the Glorious Revolution. The distance between its style and thought and the style and thought of the Neo-Classic critics makes plain, if any evidence were needed, how completely cut off from

10 See Aubrey, *Brief Lives*, ed. Clarke, vol. II, p. 304.
11 cf. F. R. Leavis, *op. cit.*, chap. I.

the ordinary publications of the time thoroughly Metaphysical poetry then was. The passage comes from an essay *Of Seriousness* in the *Miscellanies* of John Norris of Bemerton, who was indeed isolated in his age as a scholarly and serious-minded man and a philosopher of unusual principles. It is not specifically concerned with wit or even with literature, and one should hesitate, though it is common in recent criticism, to say that a writer means something different from what he says. Nevertheless I feel justified in lifting it out of its context and reinterpreting it in a more particular way than Norris presumably intended. He has discussed the relationship between seriousness and wisdom in the deepest sense and sums up:

> For a Man to pretend to work out a neat Scheme of Thoughts with a maggotty unsettled Head, is as ridiculous and nonsensical, as to think to write *straight* in a jumbling Coach, or to draw an exact Picture with a Palsie Hand. . . .
>
> But because a solemn Deportment may sometimes disguise an unthinking Mind, and *Grave* in some Men's Dictionaries, signifie the same as *Dull*, I shall put the Character a little home, and define more closely wherein the true idea of Seriousness consists or what it is to be in good earnest, a *serious Man*.
>
> And First, I shall remove it from the neighbourhood of those things, which by their symbolizing with it in outward appearance, prove oftentimes the occasion of Mistake and Confusion. It does not therefore consist in the Morosity of a Cynic, nor in the Severity of an *Ascetic*, nor in the Demureness of a *Precisian*, nor in the Deadness and Sullenness of a *Quaker*, nor in the solemn Mien of an Italian, nor in the slow pace of a *Spaniard*: 'Tis neither in a drooping Head, nor a Mortify'd Face, nor a Primitive Board.
>
> 'Tis something very different, and much more Excellent than all this, that must make up a serious Man. And I believe I shall not misrepresent him, if I say, he is one that duly and impartially weighs the moments of Things, so as neither to value Trifles, nor despise Things really Excellent: That dwells much at *home*, and studies to know himself as well as Books and Men. . . . In a word That knows how to distinguish between a Moment and Eternity. This is to be truely *serious*: and however the Pretender to gaiety and lightsomeness of Humour may miscall and ridicule it by the Names of Melancholy, Dullness, and Stupidity, etc. He that is thus affected cannot miss of being Wise and Good here, and Happy hereafter. And 'Twill be *his* turn to *Laugh* when others shall *Mourn* and *Weep*.

Norris writes as a moral controversialist from his isolated position between Dissent and Restoration society — later he did not even get on with his Bishop of Salisbury, the tolerant Burnet — but I find a more immediate relevance in his words for literary purposes. This obscure don seems to have detached himself sufficiently to look back over an epoch and attempt to define the quality of its mind. With a little reflection and attention to others' statements and examples, one realizes that the tradition of wit in poetry is the outcome of this kind of 'seriousness', this scrupulous and lively sense of values. I am reminded of Davenant's description of wit rather than Dryden's, but Norris has a better-trained mind than the former. Also, he was just far enough away from his theme to be detached, but near enough to see it clearly. In this respect he has the advantage over Mr Eliot in what seems like a curious anticipation of the Marvell essay and of

> Wit is related to other meanings of the word, and even to that which connotes mirth — though there especially, perhaps, to what is most alien to our age, a holy mirth.[12]

This interpretation would place Norris in an important and interesting position, and would give him a second claim to our attention as at least a potential critic, of one brilliant *aperçu*, who joins the small company of those who wrote useful explanations of the elusive spirit of wit. I suggest that, besides embodying the Metaphysical manner in a vigorous and personal way, he also, consciously or unconsciously, understood the spirit of that poetry and expressed it in memorable words. It is, of course, obviously impossible to separate the creative imagination of any age from its wider intellectual and emotional qualities. We have seen how earlier descriptions of wit are related to the habits of mind of the times, and that Davenant at least in his muddled way attempts to adumbrate something more that a merely literary conception. Modern critics have done likewise. It would therefore be very satisfactory if one could take these paragraphs of Norris, one of the last Metaphysicals, as valid in both the general and the particular application. One then has a comprehensive series of documents which correspond by their fullness with what later critics, with their wider purview and clearer sense of proportion, have seen and also have that extra authority which contemporary witness gives.

12 *Note on two Odes of Cowley, XVIIth Century Studies presented to Sir Herbert Grierson,* p. 242.

2

THE TONE OF BEN JONSON'S POETRY

IT IS WELL KNOWN that Pope imitated the opening couplet of Jonson's *Elegie on the Lady Jane Pawlet, Marchion: of Winton*:

> What gentle ghost, besprent with *April* deaw,
> Hayles me, so solemnly, to yonder Yewgh?

in his own opening couplet of the *Elegy to the Memory of an Unfortunate Lady*:

> What beck'ning ghost, along the moonlight shade
> Invites my steps, and points to yonder glade?

The similarity and the difference between the grand style of Pope and the slightly Spenserian language of Jonson on this occasion are obvious. I have chosen to begin with a reference to this piece of plagiarism, however, because these two poems may be taken to mark, in so far as there are any beginnings and ends in literature, the limits of my study, and because the debt draws pointed attention to the dignified and courteous tone of Jonson's poetry, especially in his occasional verses. Several lines of elegy, which often intersect and blend, run between Jonson's epitaphs and formal eulogies and Pope's poem, which seems to gather up into itself all the various threads, the earlier Metaphysical and philosophic meditation of Donne, the formality of Cowley on Crashaw, the tenderness of Cowley on Hervey, the satire of Dryden in the ode on Anne Killigrew and the elegiac of Milton on the same Lady Jane.[1] Pope inherited a large measure of Metaphysical wit coming from Donne, but the predominant aspect of his genius, the Augustan decorum, can be traced back to Donne's contemporary, Jonson.

1 Dr F. R. Leavis has analysed the Pope's poem in *Revaluation*, chap. III.

Although Jonson's greatness as a poet is generally recognized, very little has been written on his lyric and other non-dramatic poems. There is room for a detailed consideration of certain aspects of this work and for some redirection of attention towards poems hitherto neglected. Making a limited approach, I want to try to locate and define as clearly as possible his characteristic tone and civilized quality.

One often finds oneself trying, with a certain sense of frustration, to reconcile Professor C. H. Herford's morose rough diamond 'with no native well-spring of verse music' and the kind of seventeenth-century Mallarmé implied by Mr Ralph Walker.[2] The coarse side of Jonson must not be forgotten. He was rooted in the English life of tavern and workshop in his life and in his art, besides being the friend of Selden and Lord Aubigny. We have to take into account *The Voyage* as well as the *Hymn to Diana*, and remember the last line of *A Celebration of Charis*. Dr Leavis places the odes to himself at the central point, as showing us both the independent, forthright working dramatist and the learned Horatian who brought out his plays annotated in folio.[3]

I disagree with Dr Leavis about the odes. 'The racy personal force' and the 'weighty and assertive personal assurance' are indeed present. The poems are eminently successful in the sense that they communicate their content without hesitation or vagueness. One can accept and applaud the fiercely contemptuous satire on dullness and ill will, but the final effect, I think, embarrasses still, as it seems to have embarrassed the 'Tribe' and as the author in person had earlier embarrassed Drummond of Hawthornden.[4] These odes are too personal and self-regarding. It is not the self-pity of a Shelley that is forced upon us, but self-assertion and unseemly pride:

> 'Twere simple fury still thyselfe to waste
> On such as have no taste....
> 'Tis crowne enough to vertue still, her owne applause.

This is not redeemed by the finer aspiration of:

> Strike that disdaine-full heate
> Throughout, to their defeate,

2 See *Ben Jonson*, ed. Herford and Simpson, vol. II, p. 340; and R. Walker, *Ben Jonson's Lyric Poetry*, *The Criterion*, vol. XIII, 1934.
3 *Revaluation*, chap. I.
4 *Conversations*, 19.

As curious fooles, and envious of thy straine,
May, blushing, sweare no palsey's in thy braine.

Though Cartwright, Randolph and Cleveland approved, one can sympathize with that excellent literary critic, Thomas Carew, when he expostulates:

'Tis true (dear Ben) thy just chastizing hand
Hath fixed upon the sotted Age a brand
To their swolne pride, and empty scribbling due . . .
. . . but if thou bind,
By Citie custome, or by *Gavell-kind*,
In equall shares thy love on all thy race,
We may distinguish of their sexe and place;
Though one hand form them and though one brain strike
Souls into all, they are not all alike.
Why should the follies then of this dull age
Draw from thy Pen such an immodest rage,
As seems to blast thy (else immortall) Bayes,
When thine owne hand proclaims thy ytch of praise?
Such thirst will argue drought. . . .
The wiser world doth greater Thee confesse
Than all men else, than Thyself only lesse.

Along with his mastery of the irregular Donncan couplet, Carew shows here a fineness of feeling and a regard for his poetic father, a polish of tone and an integrity of character, which represent all that was best in the class and way of life from which he came. Carew feels that the great intellectual leader has been ungentlemanly in a very deep sense; that ideal demanded a measure of humility; it was something rooted in the traditional code and which became obliterated in the more superficial, if more formally polite, Augustan age. In an ode on the same theme, not published until the present century, Jonson expresses a proud but far more admirable attitude towards the public:

Yet since the bright and wise
Minerva deignes
Uppon this humbled earth to cast hir eyes,
Wee'l rip our ritchest veynes
And once more strike the Eare of tyme with those fresh straynes:
As shall besides delight
And Cuninge of their grounde

Give cause to some of wonder, some despight;
But unto more despaire to imitate their sounde. . . .

Cast reverence if not feare
Throughout their generall brests
And by their taking let it once appeare
Who worthie come, who not, to be witts Pallace guests.

However, the point to be emphasized is that Jonson at his best has a superlatively civilized tone, and it was, in fact, in him that Carew found models for the expression of such a tone in poetry. In Jonson it springs, of course, mainly from his classical culture, that culture which Carew and his class shared in a way corresponding to Jonson's participation in the social activities which produced the manners and the tone of their world. The tone which issues in Jonson's poetry from this double source is best exemplified in the following ode:

High-spirited friend,
I send nor Balmes, nor Cor'sives to your wound,
Your fate hath found
A gentler, and more agile hand, to tend
The Cure of that, which is but corporall,
And doubtful Dayes, (which were nam'd *Criticall,*)
Have made their fairest flight,
And now are out of sight.
Yet doth some wholesome Physick for the mind,
Wrapt in this paper lie,
Which in the taking if you misapply
You are unkind.

Your covetous hand,
Happy in that faire honour it hath gain'd
Must now be rayn'd.
True valour doth her owne renowne command
In one full Action; nor have you now more
To doe, then to be husband of that store.
Thinke but how deare you bought
This same which you have caught,
Such thoughts wil make you more in love with truth.
'Tis wisdom, and that high
For men to use their fortune reverently,
Even in youth.

This is no mere pindaric experiment. To whoever is addressed Jonson is giving extremely intimate personal advice, analysing a situation and a character instead of writing a conventional epithalamium, but his delicate movement and hesitating phrases, using the opportunities of the formal pattern, keep it free of all suggestion of patronage or importunity. There is great strength in the total effect of mature wisdom. Jonson is appealing to an ideal of human dignity and reasonable behaviour held in common with his reader which inspires frankness and at the same time sincere mutual respect. The ultimate basis is again the old idea of courtesy. This was a quality of the spirit which made it possible to consider serious moral matters in a social context without losing sight of their seriousness or doing anything in what would later be called 'bad form'. This ode by itself seems to me a refutation of Professor Herford's opinion that Jonson 'for all his generous warmth lacked the finer graces of familiarity'. It has both.

The wit of Jonson, like that of Donne, manifests itself in many ways. As an intellectual force it has a disciplinary and clarifying rather than a free-ranging and elaborating effect,[5] but the relationship between the two poets is shown in Jonson's admiration for Donne and in the common features of that group of elegies whose authorship has long been in dispute between them.[6] In discussing the more social aspect of Jonson's wit, the tone that he handed on to his 'sons', usually in the form of an economy and polish of technique, I think that one can claim that these 'finer graces' form one of Jonson's great qualities as a poet. 'High-spirited friend . . . ' and 'Fair friend . . .'[7] that elegant, but closely reasoned and firmly phrased lyric, equally expressive of his distinctive classical urbanity, together give us the quintessence of Jonson's attitude towards his friends and fellow poets, his patrons and patronesses. It is not the formal decorum of a large polite world — such, in any case, did not yet exist — but one feels it to be, I think, the tone of small circles

5 See the discussion of wit in chap. I.

6 Praise outweighs blame in the *Conversations*, and, if one takes these remarks along with the two epigrams to the poet and that to Lady Bedford 'with Mr Donne's Satires', the whole forms a brief but apposite critical estimate.

With regard to the disputed authorship of the four elegies, I think that Mrs Simpson gives good reasons for what should be a final division of responsibility, allotting *The Expostulation* to Donne and the others to Jonson (*Jonson and Donne*, *R.E.S.*, vol. XV).

7 Professor Herford and Mr and Mrs Simpson give this poem to Godolphin (*Ben Jonson*, vol. VIII, p. 265). If it is his, it not only shows his distinction as a poet, but also the remarkable homogeneity of tone within the 'Tribe'.

in which aristocratic and cultivated people knew each other intimately. One can back up these deductions by a short survey of Jonson's occasional and certain other verses and of imitations by his 'sons'. They have the kind of tone I have just noted, and they describe the life that contributed to produce that tone. Beside these poems much of the social verse, even of Pope, sounds brassy. One knows that life at Whitehall, particularly in the reign of James I, was often disorderly, not to say squalid, and that sports and pastimes on the best-ordered country estate were rough and cruel, but the refinement was also there, sometimes in the same people. In the poetry it is preserved for ever.

The epigram, *Inviting a Friend to Supper*, is admirable social verse, besides being a document of the Jonson world, an offering of scholarly conversation with simple but good food and wine—Virgil and Tacitus with canary. A long series of epigrams and complimentary verses sketch in the type of men with whom Jonson liked to associate and the qualities that for him made up a civilized life. *An Epistle, answering one that asked to be Sealed of the Tribe of* BEN is unfortunately little more than satire on smart London life and the masques of Inigo Jones. *An Epistle to a Friend, to persuade him to the Warres* with its finely realized opening:

> Wake, friend, from forth thy Lethargie: the Drum
> Beates brave and loude in *Europe* and bids come
> All that dare rowse . . .

is again mainly negative, a vigorous and racy denunciation of loose sexual morality and excessive drinking, but the ending sets up a heroic ideal of moral and physical valour, temperate, stoical and devout, the very reverse of the Renaissance braggart:

> Goe, quit 'hem all. And take along with thee
> Thy true friends wishes, *Colby*, which shall be
> That thine be just, and honest; that thy Deeds
> Not wound thy conscience, when thy body bleeds;
> That thou dost all things more for truth, then glory
> And never but for doing wrong be sory
> That by commanding first thyselfe, thou mak'st
> Thy person fit for any charge thou tak'st;
> That fortune never make thee to complaine,
> But what shee gives, thou dar'st give her againe;

That whatsoever face thy fate puts on,
Thou shrinke or start not, but be always one;
That thou thinke nothing great, but what is good,
And from that thought strive to be understood.
So, 'live so dead, thou wilt preserve a fame
Still pretious, with the odour of thy name.
And last, blaspheme not, we did never heare
Man thought the valianter, 'cause he durst sweare. . . .

The two poems to the brilliant young Earl of Newcastle, exalting his horsemanship and his fencing, show a kindred enthusiasm. As Professor Herford remarks, admiration for virility 'gives eloquence to his verse'. Vincent Corbet stands for graver and gentler virtues:

His Mind was pure, and neatly kept,
As were his Nourceries; and swept
So of uncleannesse, or offence,
That never came ill odour thence:
And add his Actions unto these,
They were as specious as his Trees.
'Tis true, he could not reprehend,
His very Manners taught to 'mend,
They were so even, grave, and holy;
No stubbornnesse so stiffe, nor folly
To licence ever was so light
As twice to trespasse in his sight,
His looks would so correct it, when
It chid the vice, yet not the Men.
Much from him I confesse I wonne,
And more, and more, I should have done,
But that I understood him scant.
Now I conceive him by my want. . . .

The poet's self-criticism emphasizes the respectfulness of his attitude and deserves particular notice in this essay. In addressing Selden his verse is less distinguished, but it must be quoted for the attitude to himself shown in:

Though I confesse (as every Muse hath err'd,
And mine not least) . . .

and for the conception of scholarship and the literary life described:

Stand forth my Object, then, you that have beene
Ever at home: yet, have all Countries seene;

And like a Compasse keeping one foot still
Upon your Center, doe your circle fill
Of generall knowledge; watch'd men, manners too,
Heard what times past have said, seene what ours doe:
Which Grace shall I make love to first? your skill,
Or faith in things? or is't your wealth and will
T'instruct and teach? or your unweary'd paine
Of Gathering? Bountie'in pouring out againe?
What fables have you vext! what truth redeem'd!
Antiquities search'd! Opinions dis-esteem'd!
Impostures branded! and Authorities urg'd! . . .

In writing to Drayton, Jonson notes that they have not followed the custom of exchanging verses and continues:

And, though I now begin, 'tis not to rub
Hanch against Hanch, or raise a rhyming *Club*
About the towne.

'Butter reviewers', said Mr Nixon to the young Hugh Selwyn Mauberley.

This quotation rounds off my references to Jonson's verses on himself as a writer and his relation to the literary world. One does not take everything in seventeenth-century commendatory verses at its face value. Drayton was no Homer, but it is worth studying what Jonson says — and, more important, does not say — about the lesser figures whom he honours. The most interesting lines in the eulogy of Shakespeare are those calling upon the shades of the Greek tragedians. Jonson's critical acumen here breaks through all his own and the age's prejudices. Sir Henry Savile was somewhat above the Jonson circle and receives a formal epigram, but the ideals admired as embodied in him correspond to those of the epistle to Selden, literary skill joined to integrity of character[8] — a very solemn conception of the philosopher and the gentleman, to recall deliberately Addison's famous phrase:

We need a man that knows the severall graces
Of historie, and how to apt their places;
Where brevitie, where splendour, and where height,

8 Courthope notes that in dedicating to Savile a translation of Cicero, *De Oratore*, Lib. II, 62-3, Jonson reverses the order of qualities, making moral strength more important than literary skill (*History of English Poetry*, vol. III, p. 181); it is typical of him.

Where sweetnesse is requir'd and where weight;
We need a man, can speake of the intents,
The councells, actions, orders and events
Of state, and censure them: we need his pen
Can write the things, the causes, and the men.
But most we need his faith (and all have you)
That dares nor write things false, nor hide things true.

One sees in these poems the positive moral and intellectual values which are more usually merely implicit in the plays; young Wittipol in *The Devil is an Ass* emerges as a personality of some solidity and life, but the majestic Cicero is never an adequate dramatic foil to the political gangsters in *Catiline*. In the poems one can observe, described and felt in the texture of the poetry itself, the cultural ideals that gave Jonson his assurance and intellectual dignity and at the same time his feeling for civilized personal relationships. His tone only fails him when personal bitterness or excessive indignation causes him to lose his bearings and his sense of fellowship in the republic of letters.

Jonson was, however, conscious of a larger community than that meeting at the Devil Tavern with connections at the universities. Some of his finest verse celebrates this social scene and the characters who inhabited it and, in fact, led the nation. Courthope remarks that in this mode 'Jonson is unequalled by any English poet, except perhaps Pope at his best'.[9] We know from the plays what he thought of the projectors and of other pioneers of nascent capitalism. He held older ideals of social justice and responsibility.[10] He saw the values he believed in embodied in certain noblemen and squires, and in statesmen and lawgivers such as Burleigh and Sir Edward Coke. The greatest document, and also the finest poem, in this connection is, of course, *To Penshurst*:

Thou are not, PENSHURST, built for envious show,
Of touch, or marble; nor canst boast a row
Of polish'd pillars, or a roofe of gold:
Thou hast no lantherne, whereof tales are told;
Or stayre, or courts; but stand'st an ancient pile,
And these grudg'd at, art reverenc'd the while.

9 *ibid.*, p. 179.
10 For the background of what follows I am much indebted to Professor Trevelyan's *England under the Stuarts*, chaps. I–II, and Professor L. C. Knight's *Drama and Society in the Age of Ben Jonson*, chaps. I–IV.

It is a medieval house — it happens to have been built about the year of Chaucer's birth. For Jonson a new genius presides over it from:

> That taller tree, which of a nut was set,
> At his great birth, where all the *Muses* met.

It was now the seat of Sir Philip Sidney's brother, and Sidney appears several times in similar poems as the representative of civilization.[11] He brings the culture of *Il Cortegiano* to bear on the more active traditional idea of the gentleman expressed in, say, Langland's:

> Kings and knightes . sholde kepe it by resoun,
> Riden and rappe down . the reumes aboute,
> And taken transgressores . and tyen hem faste,
> Till treuthe had ytermyned . her trespas to ende,
> That is the profession appertly . that appendeth for knightes,
> And nought to fasten on Fryday . in fyvescore wynter,
> But holden with him and with her . that wolden al treuthe,
> And never leue hem for loue . ne for lacchyng of syluer.[12]

Penshurst is surrounded by all the beauty and wealth of nature, but it is much more than a house:

> And though thy walls be of the countrey stone,
> They'are rear'd with no mans ruine, no mans grone,
> There's none, that dwell about them, wish them downe. . . .
> Where comes no guest, but is allow'd to eate,
> Without his feare, and of thy lords own meate:
> Where the same beere, and bread, and self-same wine,
> That is his Lordships, shall be also mine.
> And I not faine to sit (as some, this day,
> At great mens tables) and yet dine away.

11 cf. *To Sir Edward Sacvile*, *To the Countess of Rutland* and *To Lady Mary Wroth*.

12 *Piers Plowman*, B., Passus I, 94-101. I am indebted to Mr Dawson's *The Vision of Piers Plowman* in *Medieval Religion* for this quotation. I quote Langland as a representative spokesman. I do not wish to suggest that seventeenth-century noblemen made a habit of reading him; Peacham refers to 'that bitter *Satyre of Piers Plowman*' (*Compleat Gentleman*, ed. Gordon, p. 95), but he may mean one of the imitations, as he attributes it to Lydgate.

In the matter of culture Peacham lays down a scheme of literary, musical and artistic studies for the gentleman and suggests a suitable blend of pride and condescension in manners; similarly Lord Herbert ends his educational recommendations: 'I could say much more . . . and particularly concerning the discreet civility which is to be observed in communication either with friends or strangers . . . many precepts conducing there unto may be had in *Guazzo de la Civile Conversation*, and *Galateus de Moribus*' (*Life*, ed. Lee, p. 42).

Jonson sees it as an active centre of a patriarchal community in which duties and responsibilities are as important as rights, and of a way of life in which all classes, including the poet — Jonson intimates that for him and for others such hospitality is becoming a thing of the past — yet live in close personal contact. *To Sir Robert Wroth* describes a very similar scene at Durance with rather more emphasis on the sporting life of the great estate — an aspect less likely to be forgotten:

> Or if thou list the night in watch to breake,
> A-bed canst heare the loud stag speake,
> In spring, oft roused for thy masters sport,
> Who, for it, makes thy house his court;
> Or with thy friends the heart of all the yeare
> Divid'st, upon the lesser Deere:
> In Autumn, at the Partrich mak'st a flight,
> And giv'st thy gladder guest the sight;
> And, in the winter, hunt'st the flying hare,
> More for thy exercise, than fare;
> While all, that follow, their glad eares apply
> To the full greatnesse of the cry:
> Or hawking at the river, or the bush,
> Or shooting at the greedie thrush,
> Thou dost with some delight the day out-weare,
> Although the coldest of the yeere!
> The whilst, the severall seasons . . .
> Thus PAN and SYLVANE having had their rites,
> COMUS puts in, for new delights;
> And fills thy open hall with mirth and cheere,
> As if in SATURNES raigne it were;
> APOLLO's harpe, and HERMES lyre resound,
> Nor are the *Muses* strangers found.
> The rout of rurall folk come thronging in,
> (Their rudenesse then is thought no sinne)
> Thy noblest spouse affords them welcome grace,
> And the great *Heroes*, of her race,
> Sit mixt with loss of state, or reverence.
> Freedom doth with degree dispense.

The Golden Age is thus naturalized in the hall of an English mansion in a real agricultural setting, and we end with an almost Homeric scene of feasting, in which bounty and humanity have temporarily overthrown the whole social hierarchy. Other contemporary moralists and commentators lamented that this old-fashioned 'house-keeping' was dying out. In Selden's *Table Talk* the account of the *Hall* is significantly in the past tense:

> The Hall was the Place where the great Lord used to eat, (wherefore else were Halls made so big?), where he saw all his Servants and Tenants about him. He eat not in private, except in time of sickness: when he became a thing cooped up, all his greatness was spilled. Nay, the King himself used to eat in the Hall, and his Lords sat with him, and then he understood Men.

Inigo Jones's Double Cube Room at Wilton, say, would not have lent itself to such a life. It may sound cheap to say that Jonson made the most of two worlds; he certainly wrote at a time when a highly cultivated society still kept in close contact with the community which supported it and still preserved traditions which encouraged it to maintain this kind of give and take, social, economic and cultural.

Nevertheless, despite changing architecture and changing habits of life, the ideal persisted. Jonson initiated an extremely interesting line of what, borrowing a modern analogy, one may call documentary poetry. It deserves a brief exploration. The most obvious imitations of his poems are Carew's *To Saxham* and *To my Friend G.N., from Wrest.* No one is going to claim that Carew shared his master's powers of social observation. The first poem is a light and fanciful thing; the other, less well known, which gives a detailed picture of the scene and of the social organization represented there, illustrates a number of points already made:

> Such pure and uncompounded beauties blesse
> This Mansion with a usefull comelinesse,
> Devoide of art, for here the Architect
> Did not with curious skill a Pile erect
> Of carved Marble, Touch or Porphyry,
> But built a house for hospitalitie. . . .
> The Lord and Lady of this place delight
> Rather to be in act, than seeme in sight.
> Instead of Statues to adorne their wall,
> They throng with living men their merry Hall,
> Where, at large Tables fill'd with wholesome meates,
> The servant, tenant, and kind neighbour eates.

Some of that ranke, spun of a finer thread,
Are with the Women, Steward, and Chaplaine fed
With daintier cates; Others of better note,
Whom wealth, parts, office, or the Heralds coate
Hath sever'd from the common, freely sit
At the Lords Table, whose spread sides admit
A large accesse of friends to fill those seates
Of his capacious circle. . . .
Nor crown'd with wheaten wreathes, doth *Ceres* stand
In stone, with a crook'd sickle in her hand;
Nor on a Marble Tun, his face besmear'd
With grapes, is curl'd uncizard *Bacchus* rear'd:
We offer not in Emblemes to the eyes,
But to the taste, those useful Deities,
We presse the juycie god and quaffe his blood,
And grind the Yeallow Goddesse into food.

The picture of the wine-press carries us away from the thoroughly English scene; it shows the Cavalier taking his eye off the object in order to classicize. But the mere fact that a man like Carew, derivative as he clearly is, recognized the existence — and the value — of such a scheme of things to the point of writing about it shows that the rather artificial culture of Charles I's court with its extravagant masques and its Italian pictures and Flemish painters had also not lost touch with its roots. Vandyck perhaps overdoes the elegance and refinement in his portrait of Carew and Killigrew, but when William Dobson paints Endymion Porter he shows us a florid country squire with beautiful laces and also dog and gun, leaning on a relief of muses and with a classical bust of a poet in the background; it is a superb and highly revealing work. Similarly Herrick in *The Hock-Cart* starts on the shores of the Mediterranean and then hurries home:

Come Sons of Summer, by whose toile,
We are the Lords of Wine and Oile:
By whose tough labours, and rough hands,
We rip up first, then reap our lands.
Crown'd with the eares of corne, now come,
And, to the Pipe, sing Harvest home. . . .
Well, on, brave boyes, to your Lords Hearth,
Glitt'ring with fire; where, for your mirth,
Ye shall see first the large and cheefe

Foundation of your Feast, Fat Beefe. . . .
With sev'rall dishes standing by,
As here a Custard, there a Pie,
And here all tempting Frumentie.
And for to make the merry cheere,
If smirking Wine be wanting here,
There's that, which drowns all care, stout Beere;
Which freely drink to your Lords health,
Then to the Plough, (the Common-wealth). . . .

As a whole it is, with its colloquial language, a vivid picture of a Devon harvest festival, and Herrick has suggested, in the reference to the plough, the deeper meaning. Lovelace shows us that he was something of a naturalist as well as a chivalrous Kentish squire in those fanciful and moralized descriptions of insects and in *The Falcon* for whom he laments:

Ah Victory, unhap'ly wonne!
Weeping and Red is set the Sun,
Whilst the whole Field floats in one tear,
And all the Air doth mourning wear:
Close-hooded all thy kindred come
To pay their Vows upon thy Tombe;
The *Hobby* and the *Musket* too,
Do march to take their last adieu.

The *Lanner* and the *Lanneret*,
Thy Colours bear as Banneret;
The *Goshawk* and her *Tercel*, rous'd
With Tears attend thee as new bows'd,
All these are in their dark array
Led by the various *Herald-Jay*.

But thy eternal name shall live
Whilst Quills from Ashes fame reprieve,
Whilst open stands Renown's wide dore,
And Wings are left on which to soar:
Doctor *Robbin*, the Prelate *Pye*,
And the poetick *Swan* shall dye,
Only to sing thy Elegie.

Whatever personal significance this may have had for Lovelace — it would seem to express a haunting regret for lost causes — its interest for us in the present context lies in his charming blend of the gentleman's knowledge of field sports and heraldry with poetic traditions — one thinks inevitably of the *Parlement of Foules*.[13] The idiom of these poems is, as Sir Herbert Grierson has put it, 'that of an English gentleman of the best type, natural, simple, occasionally careless, but never diverging into vulgar colloquialism . . . or into conventional, tawdry splendour'.[14] Several contributors to *Jonsonus Virbius* make plain the influence of Jonson in favour of 'right and natural language'. This is a stream of English poetry, the gentleman writing as a gentleman about his position and responsibilities, his interests and pleasures, which, if we omit Byron who is in any case often both vulgar and tawdry, now for better or worse dries up.

Early Stuart governments made several attempts to arrest the decay of the patriarchal household and the drift to London. Sir Richard Fanshawe wrote *An Ode, upon His Majesties Proclamation in the Year* 1630. *Commanding the Gentry to reside upon their Estates in the Countrey.* He sees what Jonson sees, and expresses the anxiety of those who realized how times were changing:

> Nor let the Gentry grudge to go
> Into those places whence they grew,
> But think them blest they may do so.
> Who would pursue.
>
> The smoky glory of the Town,
> That may go till his native Earth,
> And by the shining Fire sit down
> Of his own hearth. . . .
>
> The Countrey too ev'n chops for rain:
> You that exhale it by your power,
> Let the fat drops fall down again
> In a full shower. . . .

One thus sees embodied in verse of considerable distinction a picture of a social order, its natural setting and its occupations, and a sense of some of the dangers threatening it. The fact that it was written by men of very varying distinction of character and intelligence

13 As regards Chaucer's position in the early seventeenth century, it is, I think, worth recalling that, though Jonson strongly discourages the uses of 'Chaucerisms', Peacham encourages his gentleman to 'account him among the best of [his] English books in [his] library. . . . He saw in those times without his spectacles' (*The Compleat Gentleman*, ed. Gordon, p.94).

14 *Metaphysical Poetry*, p. xxxi.

sake, and for mine. He that doth them meerly for his owne sake, is like one that feeds his Cattell to sell them: he hath his Horse well drest for *Smithfield.*

Good manners for Jonson were something that, while adorning the upper tiers of the social hierarchy, should yet permeate through it. He expected the same kind of consideration from a patron as he showed towards his 'high-spirited friend', and he admired similar qualities in his friends in every sense.

The grace of Jonson's manner comes out in his addresses to noble ladies, especially the Countesses of Rutland, Montgomery, and Bedford, and Lady Mary Wroth. A consideration of them will form a conclusion to this study, for, though he flatters splendidly, he does not cringe. There were certain fixed viewpoints in Jonson's outlook.

He praises his patronesses partly for their beauty and their taste, partly for deeper qualities. He writes to Lady Mary Wroth with full Renaissance exuberance:

Madame, had all antiquitie beene lost,
    All historie seal'd up, and fables crost;
That we had left us, nor by time, nor place,
    Least mention of a *Nymph*, a *Muse*, a *Grace*,
But even their names were to be made a-new,
    Who could not but create them all, from you?
He, that but saw you weare the wheaten hat,
    Would call you more than CERES, if not that:
And, drest in shepherds tyre, who would not say:
    You were the bright OENONE, FLORA, or *May?*
If dancing, all would cry th'*Idalian* Queene,
    Were leading forth the *Graces* on the greene:
And, armed for the chase, so bare her brow
    DIANA' alone, so hit, and hunted so.

Lady Montgomery is a new Susanna, and in Lady Bedford he bows before qualities of character which belong peculiarly to his own vision:

This morning, timely rapt with holy fire,
    I thought to forme unto my zealous *Muse*,
What kind of creature I could most desire,
    To honor, serve, and love; as *Poets* use.
I meant to make her faire, and free, and wise,
    Of greatest bloud, and yet more good then great;

I meant the day-starre should not brighter rise,
Nor lend like influence from his lucent seat.
I meant she should be curteous, facile, sweet,
Hating that solemne vice of greatnesse, pride;
I meant each softest vertue, there should meet,
Fit in that softer bosome to reside.
Onely a learned, and a manly soule
I purpos'd her; that should, with even powers,
The rock, the spindle, and the sheeres controule
Of destinie, and spin her owne free houres.
Such when I meant to faine, and wish'd to see,
My *Muse* bad, *Bedford* write, and that was shee.

This beautifully polished epigram is a suitable vehicle for the presentation of a vision of aristocratic elegance, charm, virtue and intelligence — one notices the emphatic and subtle rhythm of the third quatrain — and the poet's admiration for them. One is reminded of the undirected, and possibly therefore more perfect, *Elegie*:

Though Beautie be the Marke of praise,
And yours of whom I sing be such
As not the World can praise too much,
Yet is't your vertue now I raise,

where the sense of the rarity and fragility of such qualities is delicately realized in the cadence of:

His falling Temples you have rear'd,
The withered Garlands tane away;
His Altars kept from the Decay,
That envie wish'd, and Nature fear'd.

The dangers and difficulties besetting his ideals of the lady are magnificently argued out in 'Not to know vice at all . . . ' and *To the World. A farewell for a Gentle-woman, vertuous and noble*:

No, I doe know, that I was borne
To age, misfortune, sicknesse, griefe:
But I will beare these, with that scorne,
As shall not need thy false reliefe.

This is the simple but dignified Stoicism which conditions of the age made both necessary and desirable. Jonson admired it in others and possessed it himself. This moral strength and perception, along corroborates, that there was no impassable gap between the world of the poet's vision and Jacobean and Caroline England. *Eupheme* on the Lady Venetia Digby is usually held up as an example of hyperbole; a passage in a quiet key on the character of the Lady, whether true to life in this particular case or not, shows, with a characteristic note of irony, a picture of deportment which would be appropriate to any of the scenes or characters discussed:

> All Nobilitie,
> (But pride, that schisme of incivilitie)
> She had, and it became her! she was fit
> T'have knowne no envy, but by suffring it!
> She had a mind as calme, as she was faire;
> Not tost or troubled with light Lady-aire;
> But, kept an even gate, as some streight tree
> Mov'd by the wind, so comely moved she.
> And by the awfull manage of her Eye
> She swaid all bus'nesse in the Familie!

Jonson himself, as we have seen at the start, was sometimes guilty of 'that schisme of incivilitie'. He probably needed the stimulus of good company to bring out the full refinement of his literary culture. But it is brought out over and over again, and was, and is, a model of its kind. It is impossible finally to separate the qualities presented in the poems from the poet's attitude towards them; social manner and manners are infectious and the one seems to have evoked the other. We should need more biographical information than we possess to take the matter further but I do not think it is base to attribute to Jonson what might be called poetic 'party manners'.

One cannot sum up an achievement such as Jonson's in a word. I have only touched in passing on his trenchancy and seriousness as a satirist and his strength and delicacy as a lyric poet. I wanted to deal at some length with his tone and accent because, in considering the meaning of wit, I believe that, though it changed from an intellectual to a social spirit as the century wore on, nevertheless a social spirit of a clear and peculiarly noble kind was present in poetry from the start and that this spirit is exemplified particularly in Ben Jonson. His poetry, even more than his plays, links seventeenth-century culture and the polite civilization of the Augustans to the better features of the medieval social order and to the half-religious ideal of Courtesy.

3

ABRAHAM COWLEY AND THE DECLINE OF METAPHYSICAL POETRY

COWLEY'S EPITAPH in Westminster Abbey, hailing him as 'Anglorum Pindarus, Flaccus, Maro, Deliciae Decus, Desiderium Aevi Sui' represents the height of his contemporary reputation. Milton is said to have placed him with Spenser and Shakespeare,[1] and Dryden looked upon his authority as 'almost sacred'. A century later Dr Johnson took him as a representative Metaphysical poet and went on to lay as much stress on his faults as on his virtues. Johnson's general estimate of the latter has not been exceeded by later critics though their interest in his work has been variously directed.

Cowley's versatility — or perhaps adaptability would be a more suitable word in his case — was indeed remarkable. There is ample evidence that he was an extremely self-conscious writer, much preoccupied by the problems raised by the business of putting words on paper. Sprat tells us that he was planning a discourse on Style at the time of his death; whether this would have come nearer to practice than a fashionable Horatian *ars poetica* we do not know, but the *Ode. Of Wit*, *To the Muse* and his prefaces certainly have a place among the illuminating pieces of self-criticism that poets have left behind them. He seems to have searched all his life for his appropriate mode of expression, with frequent partial but never complete success. His versatility was of a kind that springs from weakness of creative talent. It led him repeatedly to produce work which so completely suited the taste of his contemporaries that they could not help taking it for better than it really was, and his lack of precision and strength also assisted, for example, eighteenth-century

1 Reported by his widow. See *Paradise Lost*, 1775 ed., vol. I, p. lxxv.

With natures hand, not arts and pleasures yield,
Horace might envie in his *Sabine* field.

Thus would I double my lifes fading space,
For he that runs it well, runs twice his race.
        And in this true delight,
These unbought sports, and happy state,
I would not fear, nor wish my fate,
        But boldly say each night,
Tomorrow let my Sun his beames display,
Or in clouds hide them, *I have lived to-day.*

Poeticall Blossomes and *Sylva* show us in fact a microcosm of Cowley.

* * *

His reputation was still great enough ten years later for Humphrey Moseley, the leading literary publisher of the time, to think it worth bringing out an edition of *The Mistress* more or less piratically in 1647; it had been written as a literary diversion 'in a warlike, various, and tragical age . . . the best to *write of*, but the worst to *write in*'. Cowley republished it with the *Miscellanies*, written mainly at Cambridge between 1636 and 1643, in his folio of 1656. We have here the main body of his Donnean and Jonsonian verse and in a discussion of it most of the chief points about him can be raised and discussed.

Cowley's Metaphysical poems are scattered up and down his works and vary considerably in quality. Some of the lesser ones have considerable documentary interest. It seems fairly certain that he composed *The Tree of Knowledge*, an anti-scholastic poem, and *Reason, The Use of it in Divine Matters* at Cambridge, when he was in touch with the Platonists and read Bacon, rather than later on, when he was interested in Hobbes's authoritarian ideas. His rationalism corresponds fairly well with the Platonist opinion that the truths of religion may be discussed philosophically, but he states a very generally held doctrine and it seems possible that he derived inspiration from a well-known and very unpoetic source. One may compare:

In vain, alas, these outward Hopes are try'd;
    Reason within's our only *Guide*.
Reason, which (God be prais'd!) still *Walks*, for all

It's old Original *Fall.*
And since itself the boundless *Godhead* joyn'd
With *Reasonable Mind,*
It plainly shows that *Mysteries Divine*
May with our *Reason* joyn

and the full title with:

> So then the doctrine of religion, as well moral as mystical, is not to be attained but by inspiration and revelation from God.
> 4. The use notwithstanding of reason in spiritual things, and the latitude thereof, is very great and general . . .

and:

Though *Reason,* cannot through *Faith's Myst'eries* see
It sees that *There* and *such* they be;
Leads to *Heav'ens Door,* and there does humbly keep
And there through *Chinks* and *Key-holes* peep

with:

> 5. The use of human reason in religion is of two sorts. . . . In the former we see God vouchsafeth to descend to our capacity, in the expression of his mysteries . . . and applieth his inspirations to open our understandings as the form of a key to the ward of a lock.[4]

Against Hope and *For Hope* are lighter but more interesting poetry, worth noticing for the lively and friendly tone which holds together the multiplicity of images, for example in:

Brother of *Fear,* more gaily clad!
The merr'ier Fool o' th' two, yet quite as *Mad:*
Sire of *Repentance, Child* of fond *Desire!*
That blow'st the *Chymicks,* and the *Lovers* fire!

Johnson admired the elegy *On the Death of Mr Crashaw* as containing 'beauties which common authors may justly think not only above their attainment but above their ambition'. It is Cowley's most considerable Metaphysical poem. His achievement is not on a level with, say, *The Second Anniversary,* but he nevertheless avoids here the weaknesses of the *Ode. Of Wit.* It is a meditation on the relation of poetry and sainthood, opening with formal eulogy:

4 Bacon, *Advancement of Learning,* bk. II, xxv.

Cowley has brought his feelings to order and harmony in a mood of rapt contemplation. He started formally, and, after working with Neo-Classic *ordonnance* through various moods of simplicity and intimacy, he returns to a rigid convention.

Cowley wrote the *Hymn to Light* in a completely different literary atmosphere and after many excursions and experiments of his own. It is a distinguished and sustained piece of writing, but the source and effects of light do not arouse any profound ideas or feelings in him, and none of his images has more than one layer of meaning.

> Hail active Natures watchful Life and Health!
> Her joy, her Ornament, and Wealth!
> Hail to thy Husband Heat, and Thee!
> Thou the worlds beauteous Bride, the lusty Bridegroom He!
>
> Say from what Golden Quivers of the Sky
> Do all thy winged Arrows fly?
> Swiftness and Power by Birth are thine:
> From thy Great Sire they come, thy Sire the word Divine.

Presumably Light and her husband, Heat, are the creators and the ornaments of Nature, but the meaning is not precise. What one is given is an awe-struck attitude towards their creativeness and power. The rest of the poem is made up of a series of pictures which further illustrate the power of light. They are decorative and conceited and merit the Victorian adjective for Metaphysical poetry, quaint. When one reads of 'Night and her ugly Subjects':

> Asham'd and fearful to appear
> They skreen their horrid shapes with the black Hemisphere

one wonders whether Cowley had been reading *L'Allegro*.[7] There might also be half-submerged memories of Milton's *Hymn*. The idea of the beneficent power of light superseding the evil powers of darkness corresponds to the effects of the birth of Christ. In Cowley light drives away into hiding 'Night and her ugly Subjects', 'guilty Serpents and obscener Beasts', 'Lust the Master of a hardned Face' and 'Ghosts and Monster Spirits'. One wonders if any of this derives from 'speckl'd vanity' and 'leprous sin', 'th'old

7 cf. ''Mongst horrid shapes, and shrieks, and sights unholy'. I am indebted to Professor G. Bullough for this suggestion.

Dragon' with 'his foulded tail' and the pagan gods and goddesses in Milton. Cowley's heat 'the lusty Bridegroom' reminds one of Milton's sun a 'lusty Paramour'. It is at least tempting to suppose that Cowley may have brought something away from his reading of his greater contemporary and admirer which re-emerges in his own poetry. This would put him in an interesting position as a forerunner of eighteenth-century borrowers from this phase of Milton's work.

These poems bear out, I think, what I have said in connection with the *Ode. Of Wit*. Coleridge described Cowley as a very fanciful poet;[8] his imagery is usually apt and often vivid, but normally he has no complex philosophic problems to communicate to us and no strongly conflicting feelings to resolve in a word.[9] One might say that whereas in Donne or Marvell the imaginative power of the poem is manifest equally in the vividness of the parts and the grandeur of the whole, in Cowley the tone and accent of the poem is of most importance: since the conceits are all expressions of one theme and one feeling towards it, one may describe them not unaptly as decoration rather than concrete realization. They play a part but it is not a very exacting one. On account of this constant slackness in the use of words, springing simply from weakness, not from any perversity of inspiration, Cowley may be said to exemplify specifically literary, as opposed to moral decadence in poetry. I think that this quality of being a fanciful poet gave him some of his contemporary reputation. He wrote poetry that was thought to be 'the thing', in the manner of Dr Donne; but it was not disturbing or difficult to read. He did what the leading poets of the nineteen-thirties did. They provided simplified versions of the technique and some of the themes of Hopkins and Mr Eliot, which those who were more interested in 'modern poetry' than in poetry preferred to the originals. Cowley is a far greater figure — he lived, for one thing, in a greater century — but the comparison is not perhaps entirely unfair. He gave his public the themes and the technique of Metaphysical poetry, but 'the central heat had died down. Less extravagant, his wit is also less passionate and imaginative. The long wrestle between reason and imagination has ended in the victory

8 *Biographia Literaria*, chap. IV.
9 cf. Professor James Smith's account of *Metaphysical Poetry* in *Determinations*, ed. F. R. Leavis.

of reason, good sense'; Sir Herbert Grierson here[10] indicates how Cowley caught the attention of another public, that which was slowly forming the new age. They also could find something congenial in his Metaphysical poems despite his 'mixed wit', and because Cowley genuinely belonged to both worlds he gradually wrote more and more in the coming manner as the changing environment brought out this other side of his nature. He assimilated the influence of science and the tone, polite *and* vulgar, of Restoration speech. Hence one reason why he was more thought of than Cleveland and kept his reputation for so long.

It is now time to turn to those poems of Cowley and of other poets which form a continuous literary tradition from the Metaphysicals to Dryden and the poetry of the Restoration.

* * *

The body of Cowley's poetry which can best be described as Cavalier is large. I include the ode 'Here's to thee Dick . . .', *In Imitation of Horace's Ode* '*Quis multa gracilis te puer in rosa Perfusus*', *The Chronicle*, the *Anacreontiques* and *The Mistress.* When one comes nearer to these poems one sees that the tone is the distinguishing feature, and in the best of them, as in the work of Carew or Lovelace, it is a refined and intimate rather than a formal social tone. We find here, pre-eminently, what Sprat calls 'the same unaffected modesty, and natural freedom, and easie vigour, and chearful passions and innocent mirth, which appeared in all his Manners'.[11] In others a new tone creeps in, manifest in a coarsening of diction and an exaggerated cynicism, which looks forwards to the lyrics of Sedley and Rochester.

Johnson's admiration for the *Anacreontiques* brings out their character and qualities:

> The Anacreon of Cowley, like the Homer of Pope, has admitted the decoration of some modern graces, by which he is undoubtedly more amiable to common readers, and perhaps, if they were justly to declare their own perceptions, to far the greater part of those whom courtesy and ignorance are content to style the learned.
>
> These little pieces will be found more finished in their kind than any other of Cowley's works. The diction shows nothing of the mould

10 *Metaphysical Poetry*, p. lvi
11 *Life of Cowley, Critical Essays of the Seventeenth Century*, ed. Spingarn, vol. II, p. 128.

of time, and the sentiments are at no great distance from our present habitudes of thought.

What Johnson found 'amiable to common readers' can be brought out by comparing Cowley's *Grasshopper* with Lovelace's. Cowley's poem is a uniformly stylized Epicurean pastoral, the diction not over-artificial but freed from all 'grossness'. Lovelace writes a very varied and personal poem, in places no less artificial, but also strongly colloquial. Cowley begins:

> Happy *Insect*, what can be
> In happiness compar'd to Thee?
> Fed with nourishment divine
>
> The dewy *Mornings* gentle *Wine!*
> *Nature* waits upon thee still,
> And thy verdant Cup does fill,
> 'Tis fill'd wherever thou dost tread,
> *Nature* selfe's *thy Ganimed.*

It is essentially literary, whereas Lovelace begins with a much more faithfully observed description in more subtle rhythm, ending on a peculiarly gentle note:

> Oh thou that swing'st upon the waving haire
> Of some well filled Oaten Beard,
> Drunke ev'ry night with a Delicious teare
> Dropt thee from Heav'n, where now th'art reard.

His classical allusions are blended with simple speech idioms, as in:

> But, ah, the Sickle! Golden Eares are Cropt;
> *Ceres* and *Bacchus* bid good night. . . .

On the other hand here are Cowley's two extremes:

> But when thou'st drunk, and danc'd and sung,
> Thy fill, the flowry Leaves among.
> (*Voluptuous*, and *Wise* with all,
> *Epicurean Animal!*)
> Sated with thy *Summer Feast*,
> Thou retir'est to endless *Rest.*

Lovelace is the aristocrat, or at any rate the Cavalier, and his good manners include easily a gaiety and intimacy, a simplicity and a robustness. One is conscious that Cowley was the friend of Mr

Waller; behind Lovelace is the spirit of Jonson and of the community that he moved in and admired. Just as Cowley, despite his association with the Falkland circle, never really belonged to the Cavalier world, so his poetic links with Jonson's kind of classicism are comparatively weak and his manner more formal. The literary community to which Lovelace belongs was, as we have noted, created in the great country houses as much as in the elegantly cultivated court which gathered round Charles I and Henrietta Maria at Whitehall. Though Cowley never took a real place in Charles II's London, he is by contrast the gentleman of the town and the coffee-house — later a frequenter of the Grecian, perhaps, rather than White's. Cowley's drinking songs were to be succeeded by, for example, Rochester's:

> *Cupid* and *Bacchus* my Saints are:
> May Drink and Love still reign:
> With wine I wash away my Cares,
> And then to Love again.

This elegant gaiety characterizes all the *Anacreontiques*, whether their theme is wine or love:

> The busie *Sun*, (and one could guess
> By's drunken fiery face no less)
> Drinks up the *Sea*, and when h'as done,
> The *Moon* and *Stars* drink up the *Sun*
> They drink and dance by their own light,
> They drink and revel all the night . . .

and

> His *Quiver* empty'd quite at last,
> Instead of *Arrow* or of *Dart*
> He shot *Himself* into my *Heart*.
> The *Living* and the *Killing Arrow*
> Ran through the skin, the *Flesh*, the *Blood*,
> And broke the Bones and scorcht the Marrow,
> No *Trench* or *Work of Life* withstood.
> In vain I now the *Walls* maintain,
> I set out *Guards* and *Scouts* in vain,
> Since th'*En'my* does within remain.
> In vain a *Breastplate* now I wear,
> Since in my *Breast* the *Foe* I bear.

In vain my *Feet* their swiftness try;
For from the *Body* can they *fly*?

He returned to this mode late in life, when he wrote the charming *Acme and Septimius out of Catullus*.

Johnson's description of *The Chronicle* cannot be improved on either as a criticism or as a further support for my argument; it is, he says:

> . . . a composition unrivalled and alone; such gaiety of fancy, such facility of expression, and such varied similitudes, such a succession of images, and such a dance of words, it is in vain to expect except from Cowley. His strength always appears in his agility; his volatility is not the flutter of a light, but the bound of an elastic mind. His levity never leaves his learning behind it; the moralist, the politician, and the critic, mingle their influence even in this airy frolic of genius. To such a performance Suckling would have brought the gaiety, but not the knowledge; Dryden the knowledge, but not the gaiety.

The following stanzas must serve as an example:

10

Gentle *Henriette* than
    And a third *Mary* next began
    Then *Jone*, and *Jane*, and *Audria*,
And then a pretty *Thomasine*,
And then another *Katherine*,
    And then a *long Et cetera*.

11

But should I now to you relate
    The strength and riches of their *state*,
    The *Powder*, *Patches*, and the *Pins*,
The *Ribbans*, *Jewels*, and the *Rings*,
The *Lace*, the *Paint*, and *warlike things*,
    That make up all their *Magazins*.

12

If I should tell the politick Arts
    To take and keep mens hearts,
    The Letters, Embassies, and Spies,
The Frowns, and Smiles, and Flatteries,
The Quarrels, Tears, and Perjuries,
    Numberless, *Nameless Mysteries*!

13

And all the *Little Lime-twigs* laid
By *Matchavel* the *Waiting-Maid*;
I more voluminous should grow
(Chiefly if I like them should tell
All Change of *Weathers* that befell)
Then *Holinshed* or *Stow*.

14

But I will briefer with them be,
Since few of them were long with Me.
An higher and a nobler strain
My present *Emperess* does claim,
Heleonora, First o'th' Name;
Whom *God grant long to reign!*

The Mistress has always had a very mixed reputation. It was more discussed at the time than any of Cowley's works except the *Pindariques*,[12] but one cannot draw any critically precise reasons for this fame from his contemporaries. His admirers thought with Sprat that in it 'the whole Passion of Love is inimitably described with all its mighty Train of Hopes, and Joys, and Disquiets',[13] and Samuel Wesley, father of the founder of Methodism, later wrote:

If he'll paint a noble Fire,
Ah, what thoughts his songs inspire,
Vigorous Love and Gay Desire.
Who would not, *Cowley*, ruin'd be?
Who would not love, that reads, that thinks of thee?[14]

On the other hand Johnson said:

> Cowley's '*Mistress*' has no power of seduction, she plays round the head, but reaches not the heart! Her beauty and absence, her kindness and cruelty, her disdain and inconstancy, produce no correspondence of emotion. His poetical account of the virtues of plants, and colours of flowers, is not perused with more sluggish frigidity. The compositions are such as might have been written for penance by a hermit or for hire by a philosophical rhymer who had only heard of another sex. . . .

12 See Nethercot, *Cowley's Reputation*, 1660-1800, *P.M.L.A. of America*, vol. XXXVII and Loiseau, *Abraham Cowley's Reputation in England*, for detailed references.
13 *Life of Cowley, Critical Essays of the Seventeenth Century*, ed. Spingarn, vol. I p. 131.
14 In Cowley's *Works*, vol. III, 8th ed. by Charles Harper.

If we turn to Cowley's own Preface, we find, explicitly and by implication, a very reasonable account of the collection as more or less conventional verses:

> . . . *Poets* are scarce thought *Free-men* of their Company, without paying some duties, and obliging themselves to be true to *Love*. Sooner or later they must all pass through that *Tryal*, like some *Mahumetan Monks*, that are bound by their Order, once at least, in their life, to make a *Pilgrimage* to *Mecca*. . . . But we must not always make a judgement of their *manners* from their *writings* of this kind; as the Romanists uncharitably do of Beza, for a few lascivious *Sonnets* composed by him in his youth. It is not in this sense that *Poesie* is said to be a kind of *Painting*; it is not the *Picture* of the *Poet*, but of *things* and *persons* imagined by him. He may in his own practice and disposition be a *Philosopher*, nay, a *Stoick*, and yet speak sometimes with the softness of an amorous *Sappho*.

Cowley tries out many styles, and treatments of his theme. Whatever basis any of the lyrics may, or may not, have had in actuality, they yield their greatest interest as examples of verse produced between the Cavalier flowering and the overblown lyric of the Restoration. *Given Love* provides a clue in:

> I'll fix thy title next in fame
> To *Sacharissas* well sung name

Cowley is setting out to emulate Waller, and, in fact, there are many points of resemblance between them,[15] although he also aims at imitating Donne. Against Dryden's gibe that he imitated Donne to a fault in affecting the metaphysics[16] should be set Sprat's opinion that 'besides this amorous tenderness, [he knows] not how, in every Copy, there is something of more useful knowledge very naturally and gracefully insinuated',[17] which is a very valuable indication of how Cowley's blend of Metaphysical wit and good manners appealed to his contemporaries. Waller was one of the last of the Cavaliers, in that his love verse has their polite and respectful tone and was written to a lady, Lady Dorothy Sidney. Lovelace makes it even clearer that his Lucasta was the successor of Stella and that the age of chivalry lived on. No one occupied such a position under the Restoration, and the following anonymous stanza will

15 e.g. *Clad all in White*. *Poems*, ed. Waller, p. 77.
16 *On Satire*, *Essays*, ed. Ker, vol. II, p. 19.
17 *loc. cit.*, p. 131.

serve to illustrate the gentleman's attitude to the 'charmer' of the green room:

> When *Aurelia* first I courted,
> She had youth and Beauty too,
> Killing pleasures when she sported,
> And her charms were ever new;
> Conquering Time doth now deceive her,
> Which her Glories did uphold,
> All her Arts can ne'er retrieve her,
> Poor Aurelia's growing old.[18]

A quotation from Jasper Mayne will illustrate — and the mor pointedly because of the insignificance of the author — what has bee lost in mere fineness of tone, not to mention fundamental delicac of feeling.

> Time is the feather'd thing,
> And, whilst I praise
> The sparklings of thy looks and call them rays,
> Takes wing,
> Leaving behind him as he flies
> An unperceived dimness in thine eyes.[19]

Waller almost always maintains the refinement of Cavalier verse as for example in *On a Girdle*:

> A narrow compass, and yet there
> Dwells all that's good, and all that's faire:
> Give me but what this ribbon ty'd,
> Take all the sun goes round beside.

But he lacks its subtlety and vigour. Cowley possesses vigour an subtlety of a sort, but lacks a certain refinement. He never sinks t the bland and insolent vulgarity of the Restoration, but, as ha already been indicated, a good many of his lyrics remind on surprisingly enough, of Suckling.

The majority of the successful lyrics in *The Mistress* are in th light Cavalier-Metaphysical mode. When he attempts any mo serious imitation of Donne, Cowley produces pretentious pedestrian pieces such as *All-over-Love*, the two poems called *Th Soul* and *Platonick Love* which owes much to *The Extasie*.

18 *Oxford Book of XVIIth-Century Verse*, p. 898.
19 *Oxford Book of English Verse*, 1st ed., p. 301.

The following from *The Soul* will illustrate these pastiches:

Her *Body* is my *Soul*; laugh not at this,
For by my *Life* I swear it is.
'Tis that preserves my *Being* and my *Breath*;
From that proceeds all that I *do*,
Nay, all my *Thoughts* and *Speeches* too,
And *separation* from it is my *Death*.

Cowley seems to have difficulty in convincing even himself that he feels in any way as Donne felt in writing, say, *Aire and Angells*.[20] There are, however, a certain number of serious poems, both resolutions to love and various blends of admiration and criticism of women, that are worth attention. *The Spring*, *The Bargain*, *Long Life*, *The Discovery*, *The Separation* and *Written in the Juice of a Lemon* are some of these. One might expect Cowley to use the motif of the last effectively at this period of his life when secret correspondence was a daily duty. He adjures the paper solemnly:

Go then, but reverently go,
And since thou needs must *sin*, *confess* it too:
Confess'd, and with humility clothe thy shame;
For thou, who else must burned be
An *Heretick*, if she pardon thee,
May'st like a *Martyr* then enjoy the *Flame*.

But one is not asked to attach deep significance to the religious images, and indeed one could not. It is a fanciful poem and everything is carefully worked out to a satisfactory conclusion:

Still, Silly *Paper*, wilt thou think
That all this might as well be writ with *Ink*.
Oh no; there's sense in this, and *Mysterie*
Thou now maist change thy *Authors name*,
And to her *Hand* lay noble claim;
For as *She Reads*, she *Makes* the words in Thee.
Yet if thine own unworthiness,
Were still, that thou art mine, not Hers, confess
Consume thyself with Fire before her Eyes,
And so her *Grace* and *Pity* move;
The Gods, though *Beasts* they do not love.
Yet like them when they'r burnt in *Sacrifice*.

20 Mr John Sparrow has listed Cowley's main debts to Donne in his edition of *The Mistress and other Poems*.

The beautiful opening stanza of *The Change* ends on a wantonly cynical note which mars the rest of the poem:

> *Love* in her Sunny Eyes does basking play:
> *Love* walks the pleasant Mazes of her Hair;
> *Love* does on both her Lips for ever stray;
> And *sows* and *reaps* a thousand *kisses* there.
> In all her outward parts *Love's* always seen;
> But oh, He never went within.

This bitingly critical attitude characterizes *Wisdom*, *My Dyet*, *Answer to the Platonicks*, *Love and Life*, *Against Fruition*, *Women's Superstitions*, and *The Frailty*. While these poems still belong to the Cavalier tradition, one is also conscious of a certain blatancy of tone which suggests that the Restoration public must have found them congenial, as indeed it did, and that they provided a starting-point for the poets of that generation. The similarity to Suckling's tone and technique is an apt coincidence, since he also was widely read in the age of Dryden — one remembers that Millamant read him and why — 'filthy verses . . . natural, easy Suckling'. It is hard to believe that Cowley wrote some of these poems; they show remarkable adaptability and virtuosity. Whether the theme is:

> The art of *Giving*, not of *Saving Lives*

or:

> *Love*, like a greedy *Hawk*, if we give way,
> Does over-gorge himself, with his own *Prey*;
> Of very *Hopes* a surfeit he'll sustain,
> Unless by *Fears* he cast them up again:
> His spirit and sweetness dangers keep alone;
> If once he lose his *sting*, he grows a *Drone*,[21]

the cynicism needs only a little formality and a little 'heartiness' to make it the spirit of Dorset and Sedley. *The Frailty* might be by any coroneted author:

> I know 'tis *sordid*, and 'tis *low*;
> (All this as well as you I know)

21 *Against Fruition*. It is possible that Cowley is here remembering Marlowe's

> Love is not ful of pittie (as men say)
> But deaffe and cruell, where he means to pray.
> (*Hero and Leander*, II)

If so, it shows that he had read up his subject even more widely than has been realized.

Which I so hotly now pursue;
(I know all this as well as you)
But whilst this cursed flesh I bear,
And all the *Weakness* and the *Baseness* there,
Alas, alas, it will be always so.

The Rich Rival, *Discretion*, *Honour* and *The Waiting-Maid* are more individual essays in the newer manner; they combine outspokenness with Cowley's quiet tone. The first makes an excellent use of the rhythm of smart conversation and ends in a superb blend of self-irony and cool insult:

They say you're angry, and rant mightilie,
Because I love the same as you;
Alas! you're very *rich!* 'tis true;
But prithee Fool, what's that to *Love* and *Me*?
You have *Land* and *Money*, let that serve
And know you have more by that than you *deserve*. . . .

'Tis that which bids me this bright *Maid* adore;
No other thought has had access!
Did she now *beg* I'd love no *less*,
And were she'an *Empress*, I should love no *more*;
Were she as just and true to Me,
Ah, simple soul, what would become of *Thee!*

Cowley was the heir to the whole range of Metaphysical imagery, and I have not been able to find many conceits in *The Mistress* that he might not quite easily have picked up from other poets. His work is plagiaristic in a bad sense. In *Answer to the Platonicks* he uses a favourite image which I do not remember in the work of a previous poet, but which has characteristic scholarly features:

Ye talk of Fires that shine but never burn;
In this *cold world* they'll hardly serve our turn;
As useless to despairing Lovers grown,
As *Lambent flames*, to men i'th'*Frigid Zone*.[22]

22 cf.
The Star that did my *Being* frame,
Was but a *Lambent flame . . . Destinie*,

and

How *Lambent Fires* become so wonderous tame,
And bear such *shining winter* in the Flame

(*Davideis*, III)

to which there is a note which gives the Virgilian origin of the allusion. Cowley was obviously as fascinated by such an idea as he was by the newer science.

The line in *The Beauty*, which is incidentally already a Pindarique ode, in manner:

> Thou *Tulip*, who thy stock in paint dost waste . . .

reminds one that he belongs to the age when that bulb was sought after not only by horticulturists but by financial speculators.

* * *

A brief comparison of Cowley's Metaphysical poetry with that of one or two other poets of his generation will further illustrate the movement of taste. Minor poets, by their very nature, provide the most useful examples for this study. Marvell, of course, demands a chapter to himself. Crashaw and Vaughan are both highly individual poets who were, significantly, unaffected by the changes in outlook; Crashaw, in any case, died before they became clearly manifest. Neither of them exhibits wit as a rigorously critical or a socially tactful process; at the same time they have no features that could be called decadent and their work does not lead on to the Restoration in any way.

Cleveland, on the other hand, is both decadent and stands at the end of a real cul-de-sac, virtuosity in words and technique for their own sake. He converts Metaphysical poetry into a brilliant intellectual game. It is pointless to ask with Johnson for realization of imagery or a consistent and unifying theme. The protest of sincerity with which, for example, he opens his *On the Memory of Mr Edward King*:

> I am no Poet here; my pen's the spout,
> Where the rainwater of my eyes run out . . .

belies itself almost immediately. A few lines from *An Hecatomb to his Mistress* will illustrate both his cleverness with words and his helplessness when he attempts to dwell on the actual theme:

> Suppose an Angel, darting through the Air,
> Should there encounter a religious Prayer
> Mounting to Heaven, that Intelligence
> Should for a Sunday-suit thy breath condense
> Into a body. . . .
> So can I not define how sweet, how fair,
> Only I say she's now as others are.

For what perfections we to others grant,
It is her sole perfection to want.

Cowley may give us Metaphysical poetry carefully freed from unevenness and varnished over with politeness, but in the love poems Cleveland's main interest is ultimately not poetic at all; one might call it sub-fanciful. As a satirist he has real merit. In support of the Royal cause he combines ingenious scurrility with bitter hatred of the Presbyterians:

Come keen *Iambicks* with your Badgers feet,
And Badger-like, bite till your teeth do meet.
Help ye tart Satyrists to imp my rage,
With all the Scorpions that should whip this age.
Scots are like witches; do but whet your pen,
Scratch till the blood come they'll not hurt you then.

Here is the passion in Cleveland's poetry expressed with force, pointedness and sustained rhythmic skill.

The following quotations from the preface to the edition *Clievelandi Vindiciae*, 1677, give one an interesting sidelight on the position of Metaphysical poetry under the Restoration:

Thus they decry his Wit and Fancy as the clown the plump oyster when he could not crack it. And now instead of that strenuous masculine style which breatheth in this author, we have only an enervous effeminate froth offered as if they had taken the salivating pill before they set pen to paper. You must hold your breath in the perusal, lest the jest vanish by blowing on. . . .

Another blemish of this monster of perfection is the exuberance of his fancy. . . .

To cure this excess, their frugal wit hath reduced the world to a Lessian diet. If perhaps they entertain their reader to one good thought (as these new Dictators affect to speak) he may sit down and say Grace over it: the rest is words and nothing else. . . .

only we will have this friendly advice with them; that they may have one eye upon . . . the Royal Society, lest they make their poems the conterbalance when they attempt to weigh air.[23]

This edition of Cleveland was brought out by John Lake, an old pupil of his at St. John's College, Cambridge, and later Bishop

23 See *Caroline Poets*, Saintsbury, vol. III, p. 17.

of Chichester, and Samuel Drake, also an old pupil and a parson. Dryden had made Cleveland a type of literary viciousness ten years before,[24] and the authors are clearly on the defensive against the critics and ready to counter-attack with any weapon available, for example the rather misplaced reference to the Royal Society! John Norris of Bemerton wrote a similar preface to his own poems ten years later.[25] One makes the inference that a taste for specifically Metaphysical poetry — not necessarily of the best quality—survived especially among the elderly and the isolated and that they felt themselves threatened by the new dictators of letters.

Cleveland's friend and contemporary, Butler, is obviously dependent on his work, though circumstances gave the latter a perhaps greater fame and made his title part of our literary vocabulary. *Hudibras*, in so far as one can separate form and content, is of the Restoration Neo-Classic world in ideas and Metaphysical in outward form. It is a very complex burlesque of minute scholarship, religious zeal, eccentricity, low manners, political subversiveness, all the bugbears of the cultivated man of the world; Butler draws on Spenser and the traditions of chivalry, the fashionable romances and the Metaphysical style, and gives all, including the style, his distinctive farcical twist. The Knight has all the vices of the schoolmen, who are by now thoroughly discredited, one who:

> Profound in all the Nominal
> And Real ways beyond them all;
> And with as delicate a Hand,
> Could twist as tough a Rope of Sand,
> And weave fine cobwebs, fit for Skull
> That's empty when the Moon is full;
> Such as take Lodgings in a Head
> That's to be let unfurnished.

Butler effects a kind of reconstitution of the Metaphysical manner by deliberately eschewing the spirit, which he does not feel, and

24 *Essay of Dramatic Poesy*, *Essays*, ed. Ker, vol. I, p. 31.
25 See p. 144 below.
cf. in this connection Drummond of Hawthornden on the new poetry of his day: 'In vain have some men of late (Transformers of everything) consulted upon her Reformation and endeavoured to abstract her to Metaphysical Ideas and Scholastic Quiddities, denuding her of her own Habits, and those Ornaments with which she has amused the World some thousand years.' Letter quoted by L. E. Kastner, *Works of Drummond*, vol. I, p. 34. Does this refer to Malherbe, as Kastner thinks, or to Donne? Surely the latter.

using the outward features to express his own rationalized and rather superficial sensibility:

> For Rhime the Rudder is of Verses,
> With which like Ships they steer their courses

does not suggest a very serious attitude towards his art.

Two other poets of the next generation, Mrs Katherine Philips and Thomas Flatman, also show how the Metaphysical tradition was losing vitality. They link up with Cowley as poets, the three writing odes in each other's honour, and they were similarly estranged from Restoration society. Mrs Philips imitates Donne's famous image in her vaguely Platonic lyric, *Friendship in Emblem, or the Seal*:

> And in their posture is exprest
> Friendship's exalted interest:
> Each follows where the other leans,
> And what each does, the other means.
>
> And as when one foot does stand fast,
> And t'other circles seeks to cast,
> The steady part does regulate,
> And makes the wanderer's motion straight.[26]

The flaccid rhythms and the frequent use of 'and' go together in manifesting the thinness of the sentiment and the superficial interest in the figure. She can do better than this in, for example, 'I did not live until this time . . . ' or 'O my *Lucasia*, let us speak of love . . . ' but it can hardly be said that she contributes much of her own to the tradition in which she writes. Flatman, on the other hand, has a distinctive personal note, for example in *A Doomsday Thought*:

> Go to the dull churchyard and see
> Those hillocks of mortality,
> Where proudest Man is only found
> By a small swelling in the ground.
> What crowds of carcases are made
> Slaves to the pick-axe and the spade:
> Dig but a foot, or two, and make
> A cold bed, for thy dead friend's sake,

26 Professor F. P. Wilson having found an earlier example of the use of this image (*Elizabethan and Jacobean*, p. 30), I wonder whether this is the last. In view of the title of Orinda's poem is there any connection with Jonson's *impresa*, as he called it? Jonson's own use of the compass image is also worth noting (quoted on p. 30 above).

'Tis odds but in that scantling room
Thou robb'st another of his tomb,
Or in thy delving smites upon
A shinbone or a cranion.
When th'prison's full, what next can be
But the Grand Gaol-Delivery,
The Great Assize . . . ?

This deals with a typical Metaphysical theme, death and the grave, but the tension is relaxed and the poet 'knows well' how to make 'all things there agree'. It is spread out, as it were, for easy inspection. Nevertheless the lines have a certain bare forcefulness especially in the fourth couplet. *For* and *Against Thoughts* are comparable to Cowley's *For* and *Against Hope*. *Death. A Song* with its double-edged ironies, achieves an effect of wit by the use of almost the bathos of conversation:

When some old Friend shall step to my bedside,
Touch my chill face, and then shall gently slide,
  And when his next companions say,
How does he do? what hopes? shall turn away,
  Answering only with a lift up hand,
    Who can his fate withstand?
  Then shall a gasp or two, do more
  Than e're my Rhetorick could before,
Perswade the peevish World to trouble me no more!

The lyrics, such as *Love's Bravo*, *The Defiance* and *The Advice*, have their links back, but are toughly cynical in the manner of Flatman's time; the last is an urbanized and sophisticated version of 'Gather ye rosebuds . . . '. The life and habits implied and alluded to are those of the coffee-house and the Park.

The Slight presents a lady of quality in a scene of smart comedy:

I did but crave that I might kiss,
  If not her lip, at least her hand,
The coolest Lover's frequent bliss,
  And rude is she that will withstand
    That inoffensive libertie;
Shee (would you think it) in a fume
  Turn'd about and left the room,
  Not shee, she vow'd not she.

This is a stage beyond anything similar in *The Mistress*. On the whole Flatman keeps the serious and the light sides of his sensibility apart and thus definitely belongs to the end of Metaphysical wit. He is a poet of the plain striking phrase and the glimpsed social scene. He is in the Restoration world and yet not quite of it.

Nevertheless, whether as poets or as personalities, these later Metaphysicals have their places in the new cultural pattern. Cowley had, of course, an unrivalled position immediately after the return of Charles II and is constantly deferred to by Dryden. If the *Elegy on Lord Hastings* has been justly looked upon as a mere string of conceits, in the mature Dryden Metaphysical imagery forms an important and invigorating element. It is clear that Butler's satire is the forerunner of *MacFlecknoe*, and Flatman's resurrection scene suggests the last stanza of the Killigrew Ode. Flatman was an F.R.S., Mrs Philips the '*Matchless Orinda*' to the Earls of Roscommon and Orrery as well as to Mr Philips and Mrs Owen. Cleveland, judging by the numerous editions of his poems, seems to have been almost as much read as Butler. Along with Cowley these poets carried the Metaphysical manner forward from the later Cavaliers and blended it with the spirit of Neo-Classicism.

* * *

Cowley was peculiarly qualified for this task, because of the poetic development just described — later to be continued in his Pindarique odes — and because from the first he had shown marked signs of the changes to come in work which stands apart from the Metaphysical tradition. The *Davideis* is the first important Neo-Classic epic in English.[27] Dryden, as already noted, was indebted to its versification, and made the description of Hell the basis for his fabulous brothel scene in *MacFlecknoe*,[28] a use of supernatural

27 See Dr E. M. W. Tillyard's *The English Epic and its Background*, p. 422.

28 cf. Beneath the dens where *unfletcht Tempests* lye,
And infant *Winds* their tender *Voyces* try . . .
Where their vast *Courts* the *Mother-Waters keep*,
And undisturb'd by *Moons* in silence sleep . . .
(*Davideis*, I)

with

Where their vast Courts the Mother-strumpets keep,
And, undisturb'd by Watch, in silence sleep . . .
Where unfledged Actors learn to laugh and cry,
Where infant Punks their tender voices try. . . .
(*MacFlecknoe*)

machinery very characteristic of the taste of the time. Rhymer thought it an almost perfect epic.[29] With its prefatory matter and notes, it is a very interesting document for the study of the influence on poetry of seventeenth-century religion and science.[30] Though, as Sprat thought, it is a 'very creditable beginning of a divine poem', we may well agree with Johnson when he says that Cowley seems to have exhausted his stock of poetical devices in the four books completed. I find another group of poems in the first folio equally interesting as period pieces and of far higher intrinsic merit. They are in fact among his most characteristic and best work. Sprat says:

> In all the several shapes of his Style, there is still very much the likeness and impression of the same mind: the same unaffected modesty, and natural freedom and easie vigour, and chearful passions, and innocent mirth, which appeared in all his Manners. We have many things that he writ in two very unlike conditions, the University and the Court. But in his Poetry as in his Life, he mingled with excellent skill what was good in both states. In his life he joined the innocence and sincerity of the Scholar with the humanity and good behaviour of the Courtier. In his poems, he united the Solidity and Art of the one with the Gentility and Gracefulness of the other.[31]

These poems express with singular completeness the personality thus described. Once again one gets a hint as to their historical position by remembering that Johnson said that, though it was utterly deficient in deep feelings of grief, yet he preferred the elegy *On the Death of Mr Hervey* to *Lycidas*; Gray for reasons of different but equal significance admired both.[32]

The Hervey elegy is more obviously personal than previous seventeenth-century elegies; even Jonson's epitaphs on his children keep within a strict convention. The first stanza evokes the required mood by the direct presentation of a scene:

> It was a dismal and a fearful night,
> Scarce could the Morn drive on th'unwilling Light,
> When *Sleep*, *Deaths Image*, left my troubled breast,
> By something *liker Death* possest.
> My eyes with Tears did uncommanded flow,

29 Preface to Rapin, *Critical Essays of the Seventeenth Century*, ed. Spingarn, vol. II, p. 173.
30 See the discussion of this matter in Professor Basil Willey's *Seventeenth Century Background*, chap. X.
31 *Life of Cowley*, *Critical Essays of the Seventeenth Century*, ed. Spingarn, vol. II.
32 See p. 118 below.

And on my Soul hung the dull weight
Of some *Intolerable Fate.*
What Bell was that? Ah me! Too much I know.

He uses his stanza to the full, sinking, after a slightly heightened description, to the speaking voice of the grief-stricken man. In the next seven stanzas he recovers his self-composure by talking about his life at Cambridge with Hervey in the idiom and tone of courteous conversation:

Say, for you saw us, ye immortal *Lights,*
How oft unweari'd have we spent the Nights?
Till the *Ledaean Stars* so fam'd for *Love,*
Wondred at us from above.
We spent them not in toys, in lusts, or wine;
But search of deep *Philosophy,*
Wit, Eloquence, and *Poetry,*
Arts which I lov'*d*, for they, my *Friend,* were *Thine.*

Ye fields of *Cambridge* . . .

Then comes:

Had I a wreath of *Bays* about my brow,
I should contemn that flourishing honor now,
Condemn it to the *Fire*, and joy to hear
It rage and crackle there.
Instead of *Bays*, crown with sad *Cypress* me;
Cypress which *Tombs* does beautifie;
Not *Phoebus* griev'd so much as I
For him, who first was made that mournful *Tree.*

By a formal figure Cowley deliberately breaks away from his personal grief and generalizes it — Johnson's objections are literal-minded. Consolation creeps in with the idea of a beautiful tomb, and from now on the increasing panegyric carries Hervey up to Heaven and Cowley achieves final consolation in the belief that his virtues and talents will there find their proper field of action. The diction, however, continues to be very close to that of prose; stanza 13 is noteworthy:

So strong a *Wit* did *Nature* in him frame,
As all things but his *Judgement* overcame;
His *Judgement* like the heav'nly *Moon* did show,
Temp'ring that mighty *Sea* below.

Oh had he liv'd in *Learnings World*, what bound
Would have been able to controul
His over-powering Soul?
We'have lost in him *Arts* that not yet are found.

The sense and feeling look forward to Dryden's *Mr Oldham*, though Cowley has not Dryden's high formal tone. The social note of his wit is of a quieter kind. It is not Metaphysical wit, for there is no element of levity. It is eminently tactful. Feeling slowly rises through four more stanzas to the highest point of the poem:

But happy Thou, ta'ne from this frantick age,
Where *Ignorance* and *Hypocrisie* does rage!
A fitter *time* for Heav'n no soul ere chose,
The place now onely free from those.
There 'mong the *Blest* thou dost for ever shine,
And wheresoere thou casts thy view
Upon that white and radiant crew,
See'st not a *Soul* cloath'd with more *Light* than *Thine*.

Even here the rhapsodic note is still subdued and controlled — it is very different from the Crashaw elegy — and the poem ends simply with Hervey pitying:

Our dull and earthly *Poesie*,
Where *Grief* and *Mis'ery* can be join'd with *Verse*.

In Imitation of Martial's Epigram is the most satisfying early expression of Cowley's Horatianism; the admirably balanced opening and closing couplets belong with the best things in the *Essays, in Verse and Prose*, and again make one look beyond:

If, dearest Friend, it my good Fate might be
T'enjoy at once a *quiet Life* and *Thee*;
If we for *Happiness* could *leisure* find,
And *wandring Time* into a *Method* bind,
We should not sure the *Great Mens* favour need,
Nor on long *Hopes*, the *Courts thin Diet* feed. . . .

. . . . .

A few *Companions*, which ourselves should chuse,
A *Gentle Mistress*, and a *Gentler Muse*.
Such, dearest Friend, such without doubt should be
Our *Place*, our *Business*, and our *Companie*.
Now to *Himself*, alas, does neither *Live*,

But sees good *Suns*, of which we are to give
A strict *account*, set and march thick away;
Knows a man how to Live, and does he stay?

Possibly the best illustration of the *Ode. Of Wit* is *The Motto*, which also received a special commendation from Johnson. This time Cowley is inspired by confident literary ambition. The bardic note which was later to dissipate itself in the Pindariques is here controlled and its strength canalized into a regular oratorical progression:

What shall I do to be for ever known,
And make the *Age to come* mine own?

he begins, and after recounting satirically his disadvantages, he strikes out in self-contained couplets each of which seems to be a stage in a great achievement:

Yet I must on: what sound is't strikes mine ear?
Sure I *Fames Trumpet* hear.
It sounds like the *last Trumpet*, for it can
Raise up the *bur'ied Man*.
Unpast *Alpes*, stop me, but I'll cut through all,
And march, the *Muses Hannibal*
Hence all the *flattering Vanities* that lay
Nets of Roses in the way. . . .

The decasyllabic line asks a rapid question or makes a tentative assertion, which is capped by the slow deliberate octosyllabic where one emphasizes every word.

Come my best *Friends*, my *Books*, and lead me on . . .

followed by invocations of Aristotle, Cicero and Virgil, again shows his critical preoccupations. Finally he binds his couplets together to form a conclusive finish and drops to a more modest tone; the security of his presiding genii and the difficulty of emulating them is deeply realized in rhythm and image:

But you have climb'd the *Mountains* top, there sit
On the calm flour'ishing head of it,
And whilst with wearied steps we upward go
See *Us*, and *Clouds* below.

Cowley composed this Neo-Classic manifesto after writing *The*

Mistress. It represents a concentration of all his powers, deep personal feeling as a poet and scholar, a rich fancy, his knowledge of 'all the variety and power of poetical numbers' and, fusing these together, the full force of his literary judgement and moral sensibility. He seems to have appreciated his own achievement, seeing that he finally published the poem at the beginning of his collected works. Besides belonging to the small group of his undoubted successes, it is also one of those poems that place him with Waller, Denham and Davenant as a precursor of the Augustan age.

4

ABRAHAM COWLEY AND THE PINDARIQUE ODE

THE PINDARIQUE ODE is one of those species of literature of which the interest is very largely historical, but as period pieces the best odes can still impress us and they provide valuable information about contemporary tastes and literary habits. They clearly satisfied a pressing need of Restoration and eighteenth-century readers and poets — or rather they were an attempt to satisfy a need, for no one seems to have thought at all highly of actual performances in this mode. Half a century after Cowley published his odes, and thus inaugurated the convention, Congreve summed up the history of their influence as follows:

> There is nothing more frequent among us, than a sort of Poem intituled Pindarique Odes; pretending to be written in Imitation of the Manner and Style of *Pindar*, and yet I do not know that there is to this Day extant in our Language, one Ode contriv'd after his Model. What Ideas can an *English* Reader have of *Pindar*, (to whose Mouth, when a Child, the Bees brought Honey, in Omen of the future Sweetness and Melody of his Songs) when he shall see such rumbling and grating Papers of Verses, pretending to be Copies of his Works?
>
> The Character of these late Pindariques, is a Bundle of rambling incoherent Thoughts, express'd in a like parcel of irregular Stanzas, which also consist of such another Complication of disproportion'd, uncertain perplex'd Verses and Rhimes. And I appeal to any Reader, if this is not the Condition in which these Titular Odes appear.
>
> On the contrary there is nothing more regular than the Odes of *Pindar*, both as to the exact Observation of the Measures and Numbers of his Stanzas and Verses, and the Perpetual Coherence of his Thoughts. For tho' his Digressions are frequent, and his Transitions sudden, yet

is there ever some secret Connexion, which tho' not always appearing to the Eye, never fails to communicate itself to the Understanding of the Reader.

The Liberty which he took in his Numbers, and which has been so misunderstood and misapply'd by his pretended Imitators, was only in varying the Stanzas in different Odes; but in each particular Ode they are ever a Correspondent one to another in their Turns, and according to the Order of the Ode.

Congreve then expounds the basic order of Pindar's odes, and having freely granted that some English stanza scheme inspired by them might quite probably be successful, continues:

Having mentioned Mr *Cowley*, it may very well be expected, that something should be said of him, at a time when the Imitation of *Pindar* is the Theme of our Discourse. But there is that Deference due to the Memory, great Parts, and Learning of that Gentleman, that I think nothing should be objected to the Latitude he has taken in his Pindarique Odes. The Beauty of his Verses are an Attonement for the Irregularity of his Stanzas; and though he did not imitate *Pindar* in the strictness of his Numbers, he has very often happily copy'd him in the Force of his Figures, and the Sublimity of his Stile and Sentiments.

Yet I must beg leave to add, that I believe those irregular Odes of Mr *Cowley*, may have been the principal, tho' innocent Occasion of so many deform'd Poems since. . . . For my own part I frankly own my Error, in having heretofore miscall'd a few irregular *Stanzas* a Pindarique Ode; and possibly, if others, who have been under the same Mistake, would ingenuously confess the Truth, they might own that never having consulted *Pindar* himself, they took all his Irregularity upon trust; and finding their Account in the great Ease with which they could produce Odes, without being oblig'd either to Measure or Design, remain'd satisfy'd; and it may be were not altogether unwilling to neglect being undeceiv'd.[1]

Congreve puts concisely what has, in fact, been the consensus of opinion on the general run of Pindarique odes and their resemblance to their model from that day to this, and his aside on Cowley is equally representative.[2] Pindar was the last subject of Humanist research and imitation, and the real vogue for the Pindarique ode

1 *A Discourse on the Pindarique Ode, Critical Essays of the Seventeenth Century*, ed. Spingarn, vol. II, p. 350 *et seq.*

2 cf. Dryden, *Preface to Sylvae, Essays*, Ker, vol. I, pp. 267-9. He, Edward Philips (*Theatrum Poetarum*, Preface, *Crit. Essays of XVIIth Century*, ed. Spingarn, vol. II, p. 265) and Cowley himself (see p. 78) make it clear that the exact nature of Pindar's odes was well known and that Cowley divagated through choice, not ignorance.

did not begin until Neo-Classicism was well established in most European countries. Congreve's censure of the licence and irregularity of these odes suggests that they were in some ways the last gasp of Renaissance literature — that they belong to the age of anglicization of the classics — rather than typical products of Neo-Classicism. When, however, one looks at Cowley's odes and those of his successors, as they are, one sees that as English poetry they are first and foremost period pieces and could have been written at no other time.

Mr Robert Shafer has outlined the history of the English irregular ode in the grand style before Cowley.[3] He is concerned with its relation to Pindar. Beginning at the other end and taking the Restoration 'Pindarique' as a standard poetic mode it will be worthwhile seeing whether anything comparable had been written in England before 1656, and drawing appropriate conclusions. Pindar was very imperfectly understood in the sixteenth century and his name was usually uncritically coupled with that of Horace. Even in Jonson one finds that the Latin poet's influence is as strong as that of the Greek. Presumably the formal pattern of 'High-Spirited friend . . . ' derives from Pindar, but Jonson, the urbane Horatian, has completely transformed it to his own purposes. Similarly in the Cary and Morison ode the influence of Pindar and again of Horace are completely absorbed into the tone and feeling of the English poet. More important, the grand manner is unforced and sustained, and there is no theatrical exaggeration or attempt at the sublime. The most 'Pindarique' thing in Jonson is *An Ode to James Earle of Desmond, writ in Queene Elizabeths time, since lost and recovered*, which opens:

> Where art thou *Genius*? I should use
> Thy present Aide: Arise Invention,
> Wake, and put on the wings of *Pindars* Muse,
> To towre with my Intention
> High, as his mind, that doth advance
> Her upright head, above the reach of Chance,
> Or the times envie:
> *Cynthius*, I applie
> My bolder numbers to thy golden *Lyre*:
> O, then inspire

3 Robert Shafer, *The English Ode to 1660*.

Thy Priest in this strange rapture: heat my braine
With *Delphick* fire:
That I may sing my thoughts, in some unvulgar straine.

This is early and amateurish work, but the amateurishness is very like Cowley's. The phrases, 'towre with my Intention', 'Heat my braine', are the kind of thing that the Restoration poets use in order to work up a 'strange rapture' in 'some unvulgar straine'. Jonson's ode is however a mere accident. No poet of his or the next generation had any need deliberately to draw attention to, or stimulate, exalted feelings. One feels justified in saying that the normal verse modes, both dramatic and lyrical, were capable of containing without strain the whole range of human feelings, even the most sublime.

Cowley began his imitations of 'the stile and manner' of Pindar in 1651 while he was helping to carry out the sale of certain Crown property in Jersey, where, Sprat tells us, he accidentally met 'with Pindar's works, in a place where he had no other books to direct him'.[4] Between then and 1656 he composed fourteen odes and he continued to produce others till the time of his death. It is now generally recognized that he knew what he was doing. Indeed his own Preface to the odes makes this clear:

> If a man should undertake to translate *Pindar* word for word, it would be thought one *Mad man* had translated *another*; as may appear, when he that understands not the *Original*, reads the verbal Traduction of him into *Latin Prose*, than which nothing seems more *Raving*. And sure, *Rhyme*, without the addition of *Wit*, and the *Spirit of Poetry* (*quod nequeo mostrare et sentio tantum*) would but make it ten times more *Distracted* than it is in *Prose*. We must consider in *Pindar* the great difference in time betwixt his age and ours, which changes, as in *Pictures*, at least the *Colours* of *Poetry*, the no less difference betwixt the *Religions* and *Customs* of our Countrys, and a thousand particularities of places, persons, and manners, which do but confusedly appear to our Eyes at so great a distance. And lastly, (which were enough alone for my purpose) we must consider that our Ears are strangers to the Musick of his *Numbers*, which sometimes (especially in *Songs* and *Odes*) almost without any thing else, makes an excellent *Poet*. . . . It does not trouble me much that the *Grammarians* perhaps will not suffer this libertine way of rendring forreign Authors, to be called *Translation*; and I am not so much enamoured of the *Name Translator*, as not to wish rather to be *Something Better*, though it want yet a *Name*. . . .

4 *loc. cit.*, p. 131.

Upon this ground, I have in these two *Odes* of *Pindar* taken, left out, and added what I please; nor make it so much my aim to let the Reader know precisely what he spoke, as what was his *way* and *manner* of speaking.

Cowley's method had been in fact practised by Chapman and the great Elizabethan translators. The Neo-Classic critics and poets established it as a regular principle, a kind of extension of Ben Jonson's precept of plagiarism, 'to be able to convert the substance or riches of another poet to [their] own use'.[5] In the Preface to his translation of the *Aeneid*, Book II, published in the same year as the odes, Denham wrote this admirable note on how the poet uses words:

I conceive it a vulgar error in Translating Poets, to affect being *Fidus interpres*; let that care be with them that deal in matters of Fact, or matters of Faith: but whosoever aims at it in Poetry, as he attempts what is not required, so he shall never perform what he attempts, for it is not his business alone to translate Language into Language, but Poesie into Poesie; and Poesie is of so subtile a Spirit, that in the pouring out of one Language into another, it will all evaporate; and if a new Spirit be not added in Transfusion, there will remain nothing but a *Caput Mortuum*, there being certain Graces and Happinesses peculiar to every Language, which give life and energy to the words. . . . And so Speech is the apparel of our thoughts, so are there certain Garbs and Modes of speaking which vary with the Times; the fashion of our Clothes being not more subject to alteration than that of our Speech . . . and therefore if Virgil must needs speak English, it were fit he should speak not only as a Man of this Nation, but as a Man of this Age.[6]

In the Preface to the *Sylvae* (1685), Dryden clinches the matter with the assured good sense and acumen with which he always deals with specifically contemporary problems:

Thus it appears necessary that a man should be a nice critick in his mother tongue, before he attempts to translate a foreign language. Neither is it sufficient, that he be able to judge of words and style; but he must be a master of them too: he must perfectly understand

5 *Timber, Works*, ed. Herford and Simpson, vol. VIII, p. 638.
6 *Poems*, ed. T. H. Banks, p. 159. Dryden brackets Cowley and Denham together as authorities on translation (Preface to *Translations from Ovid's Epistles*, *Essays*, Ker, vol. I, p. 239).

his authors tongue, and absolutely command his own: so that to be a thorough translator, he must be a thorough poet.[7]

Cowley's aim was, in Dr Johnson's words, 'not to write as Pindar would not have written'. His conception of his undertaking was sufficiently vivid for him to embody it in an actual ode, *To the Muse*, which seems to me to tell us more about the odes than *The Resurrection* which Cowley himself holds up as an example. The first stanza lists the various features of a poem in a very different spirit from that of the *Ode. Of Wit*:

Go, the rich *Chariot* instantly prepare;
The *Queen*, my *Muse*, will take the air;
Unruly *Phansie*, with strong *Judgement* trace,
Put in nimble-footed *Wit*,
Smooth-pac'ed *Eloquence* joyn with it,
Sound *Memory* with Young *Invention* place,
Harness all the *winged race*.
Let the *Postillion Nature* mount, and let
The *Coachman Art* be set.
And let the airy *Footmen* running all beside,
Make a long row of *goodly pride*.
Figures, Conceits, Raptures and *Sentences*
In a well-ordered *dress*.
And *innocent Loves*, and *pleasant Truths*, and *useful Lies*,
In all their gaudy *Liveries*.
Mount, glorious *Queen*, thy *travelling Throne*,
And bid it to put on;
For *long*, though *chearful* is the *way*,
And *Life*, alas, allows but one ill *winters Day*.

Most of the terms of Restoration criticism are here, but without the decorum which presides over *Of Wit*. Though 'Phansie' is controlled by 'Judgement' and 'Nature' by 'Art', they are followed by 'Figures', 'Conceits' and 'Raptures' — 'useful Lies' refers again to the kind of poetic licences commented on in the notes to the *Davideis*. The later stanzas develop the new conception:

Where never *Foot* of *Man*, or *Hoof* of *Beast*,
The passage prest,
Where never *Fish* did *fly* . . .

7 *loc. cit.*, vol. I, p. 254. cf. Roscommon, *Essay on Translated Verse, Critical Essays of the Seventeenth Century*, ed. Spingarn, vol. II, p. 297, for a similar view.

Whatever *God* did *Say*,
Is all thy plain and smooth, uninterrupted *way*.
Nay ev'n beyond his *works* thy *Voyages* are known.
Thou'hast thousand *worlds* too of thine *own*,
Thou speakst, great *Queen*, in the same *stile* as *He*,
And a *New World* leaps forth when *Thou* say'st, *Let it Be*. . . .

Nay thy *Immortal Rhyme*
Makes this one short *Point* of *Time*
To fill up half the *Orb* of *Round Eternity*.

This is a decidedly more 'creative' theory of writing verse than is envisaged in Dryden's careful analysis of 'Wit-writing',[8] but the piled-up phrases and domineering accent protest too much. One is expected to feel that:

The poet here must be indeed inspir'd,
With Fury too, as well as Fancy Fir'd

slightly to twist Buckinghamshire's sense.[9] But though Neo-Classic rules may be in abeyance they are still not completely jettisoned. Cowley's notes to the odes show a preoccupation with the 'natural',[10] and with correctness of rhymes.[11] The first note to the ode *The 34 Chapter of the Prophet Isaiah* is even more indicative of his predisposition towards clarity and orderliness; after comparing Pindar's odes to the Books of the Old Testament and especially Isaiah, he goes on:

The design of it to me seems . . . to illustrate these confusions by the similitude of them to those of the last Day, though in the Text there be no Transition from the *subject* to the *similitude*; for the old fashion of writing, was like *Disputing* in *Enthymemes*, where half is left out to be supplyed by the Hearer: ours is like *Syllogisms*, where all that is meant is exprest.

He gets as near as he ever got to 'the fashion of writing' in his first two odes, imitations of the Second Olympic and the Nemeaean Odes of Pindar. He says in the Introduction to the first that 'the Ode . . . consists more in *Digressions*, than in the main subject; And the *Reader* must not be choqued to hear him speak so often of

8 See p. 16 below.
9 *An Essay Upon Poetry*, Spingarn, *op. cit.*, vol. II, p. 289.
10 *Second Olympique Ode*, st. 1, note 2. *Poems*, ed. Waller, p. 163.
11 *To Dr Scarborough*, st. 2, note 2, *loc. cit.*, p. 200.

his own *Muse*; for that is a Liberty which this kind of *Poetry* can hardly live without'. It begins thus:

> *Queen* of all Harmonious things,
> *Dancing Words* and *Speaking Strings.*
> What *God*, what *Hero* wilt thou sing?
> What happy *Man* to *equal* glories bring?
> Begin, begin thy noble choice,
> And let the Hills around reflect the *Image* of thy *Voice.*
> *Pisa* does to Jove belong,
> *Jove* and *Pisa* claim thy Song. . . .

The rhetorical questions here seem faked and pointless;[12] it affects one no more than does the later *Christ' Passion* where the vulgarer kind of Restoration elisions render Cowley's desperate ecstasy entirely ridiculous:

> Enough, my Muse, of Earthly things,
> And inspirations but of wind,
> Take up thy Lute and to it bind
> Loud and everlasting strings;
> And on 'em play, and to 'em sing
> The happy mournful stories,
> The Lamentable glories
> Of the great Crucified King.

Once in the *Second Olympique Ode* there is a tolerable passage where Cowley evokes a vision of:

> *The Muse-discovered World of Islands Fortunate*

but elsewhere these 'Pindaric' pindariques are clumsy hotch-potches to which Johnson's criticism on the ground of incongruities very aptly applies. The Pindaric invocation of the Muse to which Cowley draws attention becomes in his own work a desperate plea for, rather than a sign of, exalted inspiration. Nevertheless he had many imitators. Sprat composed his astounding medley of 'horrifics', *The Plagues of Athens*, on the model of Cowley's *Plagues of Egypt*, and there is an element of sheer melodrama in many of the great ceremonial odes of the Restoration.

12 As Cowley's version is fairly close to the original Greek, I must stress that my criticisms of this poem and of the Nemeaean Ode are intended to apply to them only as English poetry. I think it essential that this distinction should be made.

The Pindarique ode is a parallel phenomenon to the Heroick play. When normal couplet-writing was becoming too rigorously controlled by 'coolness and discretion', I believe that the Heroick play was manufactured in an attempt to give expression to feelings otherwise repressed, and similarly writers attempted, by means of 'the gaudy and inane phraseology' of the ode, to give direct and easy outlet to moods of ecstasy and enthusiasm. In almost all cases from Cowley to Gray the result is a patent fabrication, a mere assemblage of parts of well-tried 'bardic' efficacy.

Cowley's most individual Pindariques are those in the manner of the first stanza of *To the Muse*, in which, whatever his intentions in the direction of the sublime and the 'enthusiastic' may have been, what he actually gives us are elaborately fanciful Metaphysical poems on a large range of feelings and ideas. '*The Numbers* are various and irregular, and sometimes (especially some of the long ones) seem harsh and uncouth, if the just measures and cadencies be not observed in the *Pronunciation*. So that almost all their *Sweetness* and *Numerosity* (which is to be found, if I mistake not, in the roughest, if rightly repeated), lies in a manner wholly at the *Mercy* of the *Reader*.'[13] *The Resurrection, To the Muse, Destinie, Life and Fame, The Extasie, Life, Mr Cowley's Book presenting itself to the University Library of Oxford, Sitting and Drinking in a Chair made out of the Reliques of Sir Francis Drake's Ship* are all more or less in this mode. *The Resurrection* 'is truly *Pindarical*, falling from one thing into another, after his Enthusiastic manner'.[14] It is a 'wild and whirling' poem in which the blending of seriousness and levity is extremely uncertain, but it gives rise to one or two comments. Stanza 2 was possibly in Dryden's mind when he composed his *Ode on St. Cecilia's Day*:

> Begin the *Song*, and strike the *Living Lyre*;
> Lo how the *Years to come*, a numerous and well-fitted *Quire*,
> All hand in hand do decently advance.
> And to my *Song* with smooth and equal measure *dance*.
> Whilst the *dance* lasts, how long so e're it be,
> My *Musick's* Voyce shall bear it companie.
>   Till all *gentle Notes* be drown'd
>   In the *last Trumpets* dreadful sound.

13 Cowley, Preface to *Works, Poems*, ed. Waller, p. 11.
14 Cowley, st. 1, note 1 of the ode, *loc. cit.*, p. 183.

That to the *Spheres* themselves shall *silence* bring,
Untune the *Universal String*,
Then all the wide extended *Sky*,
And all th'*harmonious Worlds* on high,
And *Virgil's* sacred *work* shall dy.
And he himself shall see in one *Fire* shine
Rich *Natures* ancient *Troy*, though built by *Hands Divine*.

The rhythms are used with a Restoration restraint to build up an effect of swelling organ notes. It looks forward to *A Song for St. Cecilia's Day*:

So when the last and dreadful Hour,
This crumbling Pageant shall devour,
The Trumpet shall be heard on high,
The dead shall live, the living die,
And Musick shall untune the Sky.

The actual resurrection stanza may also have been a source of inspiration to others, for example:

Then shall the scattered *Atomes* crowding come
Back to their *Ancient Home*,
Some from *Birds*, and *Fishes* some,
Some from *Earth*, and some from *Seas*,
Some from *Beasts* and some from *Trees*,
Some descend from *Clouds* on high,
Some from *Metals* upward fly,
And where th'*attending Soul* naked, and shivering stands,
Meet, salute, and joyn their hands.
As disperst *Souldiers* at the *Trumpet's* call
Hast to their *Colours* all.

One thinks of the last stanza of Dryden's Killigrew Ode:

(When rattling Bones together fly
From the four Corners of the Skie) . . .

but a more regular user of this manner was, as has been already noted, Thomas Flatman.[15] A little later one finds the manner in Norris of Bemerton, for example, in *The Prospect*. Cowley's verse shows yet again his interest in ideas, but the Lucretian materialism did not make a profound impression on him, or he could never have

15 See p. 67 above.

mixed it so superficially with Christian eschatology. He merely makes use of both to create a serio-comic scene. Hobbes is in a similar way the influence behind *Destinie*:

> *Strange* and *Unnatural!* lets stay and see
> This *Pageant* of a *Prodigie.*
> Lo, of themselves, th'enliven'd *Chesmen* move,
> Lo, the unbred, ill-organ'd *Pieces* prove,
> As full of *Art* and *Industrie,*
> Of *Courage* and of *Policie,*
> As *we our selves* who think, ther's nothing *Wise* but *We.*
> Here a proud *Pawn* I admire
> That still advancing higher
> A top of all became
> Another *Thing* and *Name.* . . .
> And, lo, I saw *two Angels* plaid the *Mate.*
> With *Man,* alas, no otherwise it proves,
> An *unseen Hand* makes all their *Moves.*
> And some are *Great,* and some are *Small,*
> Some climb to *good,* some from *good Fortune* fall,
> Some Wisemen, and some *Fools* we call,
> *Figures,* alas, of *Speech,* for *Desti'ny plays us all.*

Again the thought is shallow, but clear and logical. The interest of the ode lies in Cowley's pleasant tone and his untiring inventiveness; it is an art of conversation kept just sufficiently in bounds by the theme to make the product a unified poem. In Flatman's words he almost runs 'the *Metaphor* stark mad into an *Allegory*, a practice very frequent and of admirable use amongst the Moderns'.[16] *Life and Fame* and *Life* are similar semi-serious arguments, the one condemning both life and fame, the other asserting a belief in immortality.[17] 'Cowley, whatever was his subject, seems to have been carried, by a kind of destiny, to the light and the familiar', wrote Johnson, reprehending his more frivolous imagery.

The largest group of Cowley's Pindariques exhibit a sublimity of style something like that postulated in the latter stanzas of *To the Muse*, but here Horatian decorum restrains excessive flights of fancy,

16 Flatman, *To the Reader, Poems, Caroline Poets*, Saintsbury, vol. III, p. 284.
17 Cowley also shows an interest in medicine in various odes, notably *To Dr Scarborough* and *Upon Dr Harvey*, from which last it is obvious that he was deeply impressed by the discovery of the 'noble Circle of the Blood'. Here he describes new discoveries instead of merely using them as sources of imagery, but both poems are too decorative to be called important manifestations of the scientific spirit of the new age.

and one finds the lineal successors of Jonson's ode for Cary and Morison and the models of the complimentary verse addresses which were presented to Restoration princes and noblemen on every kind of occasion by a necessitously obsequious race of poets and poetasters. The following belong in the main to this group: *To Mr Hobs, Brutus, To Dr Scarborough, On Orinda's Poems, Upon the occasion of a Copy of Verses of My Lord Broghills, Upon the Death of the Earl of Balcarres, Upon Dr Harvey, The Complaint, On the Death of Mrs Katherine Philips, To the Royal Society* and the odes included in the *Essays*. Here, if anywhere, Sprat's curious compliment becomes applicable: 'But that for which . . . this inequality of number is chiefly to be preferr'd, is its near affinity with prose. . . . And withall it is so large and free, that the practise of it will only exalt, not corrupt our Prose: which is certainly the most useful kind of Writing of all others: for it is the style of all business and conversation.'[18] The verse which the prose celebrant of the Royal Society admired does not differ so very greatly from the more grandiose passages of his own *History*; neither kept consistently to a 'mathematical plainness'. Though less individual to Cowley than those I have just described, these occasional odes include some of his most satisfactory verse and it is easy to see why his contemporaries and successors admired them so highly. The second stanza of *To Mr Hobs*, a poem which Mr Eliot has praised for its peculiar 'adequacy' and unforced dignity,[19] will illustrate their quality:

> Long did the mighty *Stagirite* retain
> The *universal Intellectual reign*,
> Saw his own Countreys short-liv'd *Leopard* slain,
> The stronger *Roman-Eagle* did outfly,
> Oftner *renewed* his *Age*, and saw that *Dy*,
> *Mecha* itself, in spite of *Mahumet* possest,
> And chas'ed by a wild *Deluge* from the *East*,
> His *Monarchy* new planted in the *West*.
> But as in time each great imperial race
> Degenerates and gives some new one place:
> So did this noble *Empire* wast,
> Sunk by degrees from glories past,
> And in the *School-mens* hands it perisht quite at last.

18 *loc. cit.*, p. 132.
19 *A Note on Two Odes of Cowley, XVIIth Century Studies presented to Sir Herbert Grierson.* I agree with his account of the Pindariques, but not with that of the *Ode. Of Wit.*

Then nought but *Words* it grew,
And those all Barb'rous too.
It perisht, and it vanisht, there,
And *Life*, and *Soul* breath'd out, became but empty *Air*.

There is just enough variety within the grand design to keep our interest; the alexandrine suggests the last gasp of Aristotle's declining hegemony. The argument, both here and in the whole ode, is clear and logical. M. Loiseau thinks that the grandeur of Cowley's Pindariques is an oratorical rather than a lyrical grandeur, that his long phrases remind one of the well-constructed prose period, and that the critical spirit of wit is always in control.[20] Unfortunately he does not discriminate between the several types of ode that Cowley composed, but his commentary seems to me excellent for the type I am now discussing. Cowley was peculiarly well-fitted temperamentally to address his friends with a staid Horatian dignity. In the last stanza he salutes Hobbes as much in the manner of a respectful pupil as in that of a friend:

Nor can the *Snow*, which now cold *Age* does shed
Upon thy reverend Head,
Quench or allay the noble *Fires* within,
But all which thou hast *bin*,
And all that *Youth* can *be* thou'rt yet,
So fully still dost Thou
Enjoy the *Manhood* and the *Bloom* of *Wit*,
And all the *Natural Heat*, but not the *Feaver* too.
So contraries on *Aetna's* top conspire,
Here hoary *Frosts*, and by them breaks out *Fire*,
A secure *peace* the *faithful Neighbours* keep,
Th' emboldned *Snow* next to the *Flame* does *Sleep*.
And if we weigh, like *Thee*,
Nature, and *Causes*, we shall see
That thus it *needs must be*,
To things *Immortal Time* can do no Wrong,
And that which never is *to Dye*, for ever must be *Young*.

Cowley's later odes are almost all of this kind. There are not many conceits, except in *Upon Dr Harvey*, and the tone is polite and formal. In many cases the first stanza or two are significantly the best, as for example here in *Upon the Death of the Earl of Balcarres*:

20 *Abraham Cowley: Sa Vie; Son Œuvre*, bk. II, part II, chap. II.

'Tis folly all, that can be said
By living Mortals of th'immortal dead,
And I'm afraid they laugh at the vain tears we shed.
'Tis, as if we, who stay behind
In Expectation of the wind,
Should pity those who pass'd this strait before,
And touched the universal shore.
Ah happy Man, who art to sail no more!

The pleasantly garrulous opening merges into a gentle elegiac, but there is no further variety in the poem and it tails off into monotonous eulogy. The weakness of Cowley's inspiration is unfortunately undeniable. Where he laments his failures in *The Complaint* one finds the remains of the enthusiasm for letters which gave life to his earlier statement of literary ambition, *The Motto*:

In a deep Vision's intellectual scene,
Beneath a Bow'r for sorrow made,
Th' uncomfortable shade,
Of the black Yew's unlucky green,
Mixt with the mourning Willow's careful gray,
Where Reverend *Cham* cuts out his Famous way.
The Melancholy *Cowley* lay:
And Lo! a Muse appear'd to 'his closed sight,
(The Muses oft in Lands of Vision play)
Bodied, array'd, and seen, by an internal Light,
A golden Harp, with silver strings she bore,
A wondrous Hieroglyphick Robe she wore,
In which all Colours, and all figures were,
That nature or that Fancy can create,
That Art can never imitate:
And with loose Pride it wanton'd in the Air
In such a Dress, in such a well-cloath'd Dream,
She us'd of old, near fair *Ismenus* Stream,
Pindar her *Theban* favourite to meet:
A Crown was on her Head, and wings were on her Feet.

'Its principal charm is that air of melancholy, thrown over the whole, so expressive of the poet's character', wrote Bishop Hurd.[21] The first half-dozen lines are indeed distinctly eighteenth-century elegiac, using the correct properties — though a little naïvely. In the heavy redundancy of 'Vision's intellectual scene', 'Bow'r for sorrow

21 *Select Works of Mr A. Cowley*, vol. I, p. 210.

made', 'uncomfortable shade', 'black Yew's unlucky green' and so on, Cowley works up and insists on his melancholy in a way similar to the more primitive repetitions of many of the other Pindariques.

Cowley's most successful ode in the grand style, and one of his best poems, is *To the Royal Society*, written at the request of Sprat and Evelyn and published at the beginning of Sprat's *History of the Royal Society of London* (1667). Here, though he 'could not comprehend in it many of those excellent hints which [Evelyn was] pleased to give [him]',[22] he had ample material, in which he was deeply interested, to feed his fancy. Again, holding up Bacon as a deliverer, he satirizes the schoolmen:

> Autority which did a Body boast,
> Though 'twas but Air condens'd, and stalked about,
> Like some old Giants more Gigantic Ghost,
> To terrifie the Learned Rout
> With the plain Magick of true Reasons Light,
> He chac'd out of our sight,
> Nor suffer'd Living Men to be misled
> By the vain shadows of the Dead:
> To Graves, from whence it rose, the conquer'd Phantome fled;
> He broke the Monstrous God which stood
> In midst of th'Orchard, and the whole did claim,
> Which with a useless Sith of Wood,
> And something else not worth a name,
> (Both vast for shew, yet neither fit
> Or to Defend, or to Beget:
> Ridiculous and senceless Terror!) made
> Children and superstitious Men afraid
> The Orchard's open now, and free;
> *Bacon* has broke that Scar-Crow Deitie;
> Come, enter, all that will,
> Behold the Rip'ned Fruit, come gather now your Fill.
> Yet still, methinks, we fain would be
> Catching at the Forbidden Tree,
> We would be like the Deitie,
> When Truth and Falsehood, Good and Evil, we
> Without the Sences aid within ourselves would see:
> For 'tis God only who can find,
> All Nature in his Mind.

22 Cowley, Letter to Evelyn, *Works*, Grosart, vol. 1, p. lxxvii, which also refers to Sprat's request.

The long descriptive period is followed by the simple adjuration, 'Come . . . ', conveying Cowley's, and the age's, sense of liberation from intellectual bondage. The solid visual images — fully and lucidly developed as in all these odes — suggest both the Protestant image-breaker and the scientific experimenter. The interpretation of the Tree of Knowledge story is characteristic of the time and would not, indeed, have been possible at any other; the 'Forbidden Tree' is similar to the 'right *Porphyrian Tree*' in his earlier poem, *The Tree of Knowledge*. In both cases Cowley tends to disparage the ultimate knowledge of Good and Evil in his anxiety to attack the scholastics who, he thought, had presumptuously and futilely aspired to it. Authority, the Idol of the Tribe, is thrust aside with a Baconian thoroughness, in favour of the more reverent worship which consisted in observation and experiment; one may compare this with the following from the *Advancement of Learning*:

> It was not the pure knowledge of nature and universality, a knowledge by the light wherof man did give names unto other creatures in Paradise, as they were brought before him, according to their properties, which gave occasion of the fall . . . [but it was] . . . the proud knowledge of good and evil, with an interest in man to give law unto himself, or to depend no more on God's commandments, which was the form of the temptation.[23]

Cowley is very close to his hero. The thought which he turns into poetry is often definitely anti-poetical; man, he says, had formerly been fed with 'Desserts of Poetry' 'Instead of solid Meats' but, as in Hobbes, 'the Mechanick way' is made a principle of art as well as science, and one finds again the self-conscious artist, the Neo-Classic critic of *The Motto*, achieving poetic realization of his beliefs:

> Who from the Life, an exact Piece would make,
> Must not from others Work a Copy take;
>   No, not from *Rubens* or *Vandyke*;
> Much less content himself to make it like
> Th'Idaeas and Images which lie
> In his own Fancy, or his Memory.
>   No, he before his sight must place
> The Natural and Living Face;
>   The Real object must command
> Each judgement of his Eye, and Motion of his Hand.

23 Bk. I, I, 3.

Sprat wrote of the Royal Society that:

> They have endeavour'd to separate the Knowledge of *Nature* from the Colours of *Rhetorick*, the Devices of *Fancy*, or delightful Deceit of *Fables*.[24]

As a final example of the scientific element in English Neo-Classicism, the simplification of language and effect in the name of truth, as well as of good manners, I will quote another of Sprat's more distinguished paragraphs and Cowley's stanza in praise of his friend's style:

> And indeed this is an Error, which is very natural to Man's Minds; they love not a long and tedious Doubting, though it brings them at last to a real Certainty; but they choose rather to conclude presently, than to be long in Suspence, though to better purpose. And it is with most Men's Understandings as with their eyes; to which those seem more delightful Prospects, where varieties of Hills and Woods do soon bound their Wandrings than where there is one large smooth *Campagn*, over which they may see further, but where there is nothing to delay, and stop, and divert the Sight.[25]

With Courage and Success you [the Society] the bold work begin;
    Your Cradle has not Idle bin:
None e'er but *Hercules* and you could be
At five years Age worthy a History.
    And ne're did Fortune better yet
    Th'Historian to be Story fit:
    As you from all old Errors free
And purge the Body of Philosophy:
    So from all Modern Folies He
Has vindicated Eloquence and Wit.
His candid stile like a clear Stream does slide,
    And his bright Fancy all the way
    Does like the Sun-shine in it play;
It does like *Thames*, the best of Rivers, glide,
Where the God does not rudely overturn,
    But gently pour the Crystal Urn,
And with judicious hand does the whole Current Guide.
T'has all the Beauties Nature can impart,
And all the comely Dress without the paint of Art.

24 *History of the Royal Society*, 2nd ed., p. 62.
25 *Ibid.*, pp. 32-3.

Cowley gives an admirable impression of Sprat's *History*, its polite balance of phrase and clarity of argument. He uses the forbidden devices of rhetoric, fancy and fables, but actually he is not very far from a 'close, naked, natural way of speaking', which he discreetly formalizes and heightens. It is at least an interesting coincidence that he thinks that Sprat has achieved Denham's stylistic ambition, as expressed in *Cooper's Hill*.[26] The ode is superbly put together on a regular and formal plan. Cowley is, as it were, making a speech according to the rules of oratory; he is bent on showing that *The History of the Royal Society*, like the Royal Society itself, is a great achievement of civilization, and he succeeds in both his aims.

Cowley's contemporary reputation was mainly based on his odes: 'so well were they approved by succeeding Authors, that our primest Wits have driven a notable trade in *Pindaric Odes*', wrote William Winstanley in 1687.[27] It was these formal ceremonial odes that Flatman, Sprat, Orrery, Orinda and innumerable others imitated so laboriously, though it was felt that:

> Bold man, that dares attempt *Pindarique* now,
> Since the great Pindar's greatest Son
> From the ungrateful Age is gone;
> Cowley has bid th'ungrateful Age *Adieu!*
> Apollo's rare *Columbus*, He
> Found out new *World's* of Poetry;
> He, like an *Eagle*, soar'd aloft,
> To seize his noble prey;
> Yet as a *Dove's*, his *Soul* was soft,
> Quiet as *Night*, but bright as *Day*:
> To Heaven in a fiery Chariot He
> Ascended by *Seraphic Poetry*:
> Yet which of us dull Mortals since can find
> Any *Inspiring Mantle* that *He* left behind.[28]

Of such a kind was the adulation offered up to Cowley's memory. Whatever was said about other people's odes, nothing but praise was given to Cowley's for many years. It is clear that Pindarique

26 cf. O could I flow like thee, and make thy stream
My great example, as it is my theme!
Though deep, yet clear, though gentle, yet not dull,
Strong without rage, without o'er-flowing full.

27 *Lives of the Most Famous English Poets* (1687), p. 183.

28 Flatman, *Pindarique Ode on Woodford's Version of the Psalms, Caroline Poets*, vol. III, p. 306.

odes, and especially his, met an important period taste. They expressed both the Restoration love of grandiose ceremony and the perennial human love of the rich and strange.

Gradually under the influence of Boileau and Rapin principles for constructing this *beau désordre* were formulated, for example, by the Duke of Buckinghamshire:

> A higher flight, and of a happier force
> Are *Odes*, the Muses most unruly horse;
>
> . . . . .
>
> Cowley might boast to have perform'd this part,
> Had he with Nature join'd the rules of Art;
> But ill expression gives sometimes allay
> To that rich fancy that can ne'er decay:
> Though all appear in heat and fury done,
> The language must still soft and easy run.
> These laws may seem a little too severe
> But judgement yields and fancy governs there;
> Which, though extravagant, this Muse allows,
> And makes the work much easier than it shows.[29]

But in 1700 Thomas Higgons still thought of Cowley's odes that:

> He who would worthily adorn his Herse
> Should write in his own style, in his Immortal Verse;
> But who can such Majestick Numbers write,
> With such inimitable Light?
> His high and noble Flights to reach,
> 'Tis not the Art of Precept that can teach,[30]

and Johnson is chary of dismissing them with 'unabated censure', though he is in a position to write a characteristic and suitable epitaph:

> This lax and lawless versification so much concealed the deficiencies of the barren, and flattered the laziness of the idle, that it immediately overspread our books of poetry: all the boys and girls caught the pleasing fashion, and they could do nothing else but write like Pindar. . . . Pindarism prevailed about half a century: but at last died gradually away, and other imitations supply its place.

29 *Essay on Poetry, Critical Essays of the Seventeenth Century*, ed. Spingarn, vol. II, p. 289. Presumably he borrowed his second line from Cowley's ode, *The Resurrection*:

'Tis an unruly, and a *Hard-Mouth'd Horse*.

Sir Thomas Blount's *De Re Poetica* (1694) contains much similar instruction (pp.65–8).
30 Ode prefixed to Herringman's 9th edition of Cowley.

5

COWLEY'S ESSAYS
IN VERSE AND PROSE
AND THE TRANSITION TO NEO-CLASSICISM

COWLEY FIRST MIXED PROSE and verse together in a single composition and I can recall no one since, with the exception of Traherne, who in any case does not link them so closely in theme, who has attempted to use the mode until Auden, in *The Orators*, and some of the Surrealist writers, who again are too different to be comparable. It was a plan peculiarly congenial to Cowley, and in every essay prose and verse are held together not only by subject-matter, but also by style; his handling of both mediums shows remarkable consistency of tone and feeling. Though it is necessary to separate prose and verse for purposes of description, it is not difficult to bear this unity in mind.

* * *

Before he came to write the *Essays* Cowley had had considerable practice in prose writing. He had progressed from the almost Elizabethan manner of his Preface to *Sylva* to the plain and business-like diplomatic letters. He had written *A Vision, concerning the Government of Oliver Cromwell*, which combines solemn passages reminiscent of Browne with others which have the cool irony and simpler vigour of Dryden, and shows great skill in the analysis of character. He had also written the *Proposition for the Advancement of Experimental Philosophy*, Baconian in both style and thought, and his critical prefaces.

Sprat tells us of the *Essays*:

> The last Pieces that we have from his hands are Discourses, by way of Essays, upon some of the gravest subjects that concern the Contentment

> of a Vertuous Mind. These he intended as a real Character of his thoughts upon the point of his Retirement. And accordingly you now observe in the Prose of them there is little Curiosity of Ornament, but they are written in a lower and humbler style than the rest, and, as an unfeigned Image of his Soul should be drawn, without flattery. I do not speak this to their disadvantage. For the true perfection of Wit is to be plyable to all occasions, to walk or flye, according to the Nature of every subject. And there is no doubt as much art to have only plain Conceptions on some Arguments as there is on others to have extraordinary Flights.[1]

One does not agree that this last prose and verse is quite as unadorned as the Bishop suggests, but that it is eminently personal, 'the language of his heart', to use Pope's phrase, no one can doubt; criticism comes to rest again and again in a reference to Cowley's known character and beliefs or a postulate as to their probable nature. Hurd rather unctuously remarks that:

> There is something in him that pleases above his wit, and in spite of it. It is that moral air, and tender sensibility of mind, which everyone perceives and loves in reading Mr Cowley. And this character of his genius, though it be expressed, indeed, in his other writing, comes out especially, and takes our attention most, in some of his smaller *poems and essays.*[2]

The taste, represented by Hurd, which was catered for by Gray and the minor eighteenth-century poets, found something very congenial in Cowley, his personal tone. The *Essays* convey to us Cowley's essential nature not only 'upon the point of retirement' but during his whole life. Though work as varied as the eulogy on Crashaw and *The Chronicle* must be taken into account in describing his poetic character, yet the kind of feelings and tone which inspired the Hervey elegy and *The Wish* do make up the greater part of that character, and the *Essays* are the final and consummate expression of it; he recognized this himself when he reprinted *The Vote*, written at the age of thirteen, in the essay *Of Myself.*

Disappointment at not obtaining the Mastership of the Savoy and disgust at the society of Restoration London undoubtedly

1 *Life of Cowley, Critical Essays of the Seventeenth Century*, ed. Spingarn, pp. 137-8.
2 *Select Works of Mr A. Cowley*, 3rd ed., vol. I, p. vii. See also p. 118 below.

contributed to the mood in which he wrote in his last years, but his completely controlled and leisurely style is not the expression merely of an embittered man, but of one who had always, as Sprat says by way of reproof, had 'an earnest affection for Obscurity and Retirement'.[3] Coming now to a more detailed examination of this prose, one can distinguish between the parts which resemble earlier writers and the parts written in his own newly created style. It happens that this division roughly separates the discussion of aspects of life which Cowley disliked from the statements of his preferences.

One might use the term 'familiar style' to describe the *Essays* as a whole, but it seems best to keep it for passages that resemble Izaak Walton and the early essayists and character writers. An unsophisticated simplicity of this kind comes out in such sentences as: 'This I conceive to have been honest *Hesiods* meaning' and 'Ye see he [Homer] did not contemn us peasants' from *Of Agriculture*. When Cowley is in full cry against the viciousness of town life in *The Dangers of an Honest Man in much Company* he slips into a style which reminds one of the *Anatomy of Melancholy*:

> What was the beginning of *Rome*, the *Metropolis* of all the World? what was it but a concourse of Thieves, and a Sanctuary of Criminals? It was justly named by the *Augury* of no less than twelve Vultures, and the Founder cimented his walls with Blood of his Brother; not unlike to this was the beginning of the first Town too in the world, and such is the Original sin of most Cities: their Actual encrease daily with their Age and Growth; the more people the more wicked all of them; everyone brings in his part to enflame the contagion, which becomes at last so universal and so strong, that no Precepts can be sufficient Preservatives, nor anything secure our safety, but flight from among the infected. . . .[4]

It is a vivid, vigorous sentence, but in his haste and anxiety to get all his feelings of anger and fear on paper Cowley soon forgets about logical syntax and writes in note form. Tone is neglected altogether in his intent to scare the reader away from evil. A more orderly and polite, yet still familiar, manner occurs in the following from *Of Liberty*:

3 *loc. cit.*, p. 141.
4 In the same essay Cowley shows a sensitiveness, rare at the time, in his horror at going to Bedlam as a form of entertainment.

> Pray, let us but consider a little, what mean servil things men do for this Imaginary Food [greatness]. We cannot fetch a greater example of it, then from the chief men of that Nation which boasted most of Liberty. To what pitiful baseness did the noblest *Romans* submit themselves for the obtaining of a Praetorship, or the Consular dignity: they put on the Habit of Suppliants, and ran about on foot, and in durt, through all the Tribes to beg voices, they flattered the poorest Artisans, and carried a *Nomenclator* with them, to whisper in their ear every mans name, least they should mistake it in their salutations: they shook the hand, and kist the cheek of every popular Tradesman; . . .

This lively piece of description leads on very aptly to the consideration of Cowley's most important debt to his predecessors, which occurs in the characters embedded in the essays. By his time character writing was out of fashion in England except for controversial purposes; Samuel Butler was almost the only contemporary who practised the art of Overbury. Cowley's portraits are so good that it is difficult to select an example; the ending of the long and magnificent study of an ambitious man, which describes the great political and literary patron of the Restoration surrounded by his suitors and dependents, and the short sketch of the covetous man show him conducting an argument entirely by concrete comparisons:

> But, the Ambitious man, though he be so many ways a slave (*O toties servus!*) yet he bears it bravely and heroically; he shouts and looks big upon the Stage; he thinks himself a real Prince in his Masking Habit, and deceives too all the foolish part of his Spectators: He's a slave in *Saturnalibus*. The Covetous Man is a downright Servant, a Draught Horse without Bells or Feathers; *ad Metalla Damnatus*, a man condemned to work in Mines, which is the lowest and hardest condition of servitude: and, to increase his Misery, a worker there for he knows not whom: He heapeth up Riches and knows not who shall enjoy them; 'Tis only sure that he himself neither shall nor can enjoy them. He's an indigent needy slave, he hardly allows himself Cloaths, and board-Wages; *Unciatim vix demenso de suo suum defraudans Genium comparsit miser*: He defrauds not only other Men, but his own Genius; He cheats himself for Mony, but the Servile and miserable condition is so apparent, that I leave it, as evident to every mans sight, as well as judgement.[5]

5 cf. similar effects in *A Vision*, e.g. the account of Cromwell piratically seizing the 'publick Vessel', *Essays, Plays and Sundry Verses*, ed. Waller, vol. II, p. 359.

The character of Senecio in *Of Greatness* is in some ways more richly realized, since it is constructed from notes of the man's actual eccentricities: 'he would have no servants, but huge massy fellows, no plate or household-stuff, but thrice as big as the fashion . . . he kept a Concubine that was a very Gyantess, and made her walk too alwaies in *Chiopins*. . . .'[6]

Imitations of those varieties of early prose which were the products of deliberate and conscious art do not occur so frequently in the *Essays*. There is a particularly obvious reminiscence of Sir Thomas Browne in *Of Obscurity*:

> But that is not to deceive the world, but to deceive ourselves, as *Quintilian* saies, *Vitam fallere*, to draw on still, and amuse, and deceive our Life, till it be advanced insensibly to the fatal Period, and fall into the Pit which Nature hath prepared for it.[7]

Cowley imitates Bacon several times, as one might expect from a sponsor of the Royal Society and one whose poetry is more than once inspired by Bacon's ideas. In the essay, *Of Agriculture*, he uses the terse antithetical style to emphasize the contrast between the life of the country and that of the town:

> We are here among the vast and noble Scenes of Nature; we are there among the pitiful shifts of Policy: We walk here in the light and open wayes of the Divine Bounty; we grope there in the dark and confused Labyrinths of Human Malice: Our Senses are here feasted with the clear and genuine taste of the Objects, which are all Sophisticated there, and for the most part overwhelmed with their contraries. Here Pleasure looks (methinks) like a beautiful, constant and modest Wife; it is there an impudent, fickle, and painted Harlot. Here it is harmless and cheap Plenty, there guilty and expenseful Luxury.

Cowley made this Horatian view of life more his own than any other part of the classical tradition. It expressed something fundamental in his nature and he also had more easily explainable reasons for adopting it. Alexandre Beljame has shown[8] how hard it was for a writer to earn a bare living in Restoration London; it is well known that Samuel Butler died in poverty and that Dryden was never well off and had to earn his living up to the last by means of an exacting series of contracts with Tonson. The culture of Charles II's

6 cf. *Ibid.*, pp. 448–9 for similar style.
7 cf. *Ibid.*, p. 348, 'and lastly . . . designs', and *Poems*, p.6, 'And this . . . *Funeral*'.
8 *Men of Letters and the English Public in the XVIIIth Century*, chaps. I and II.

London was coextensive with the social round, which cramped and coarsened culture, society being what it was, as much as it strengthened and refined society. One must be careful not to denigrate the later period unduly by exalting the earlier. If, for example, Carew's *To Saxham* shows the best of the Cavalier world, Rochester's satires show, no doubt, the worst of Charles II's England. It may have been necessary for Jonson to draw up his *Leges Conviviales* for the Devil Tavern. But, though a more formal code grew up in the coffee-houses, the lapses from it became decidedly more barbarous. The small aristocratic circles disappeared or became unimportant — Temple and the Newcastles spent most of their time out of London, and they were also out of the main current of civilization. The coffee-house was a microcosm of society; 'coffee-houses [made] all sorts of people sociable; the rich and poor [met] together, as also did the learned and the unlearned . . . ';[9] and there were innumerable coffee-houses. Together they made the 'Town'. The 'Town' imposed a general code of social intercourse which was more specifically urbane than that of the Cavaliers, but also necessarily less intimate and sensitive. Along with the good manners went a vulgarity which was an aspect of the snobbishness which animated, for example, the 'wit's' feeling of superiority over the 'cit'. A cultivated man could not feel really at home in that world. Evelyn expresses his disgust at 'an age so universally depraved among our wretched nobility',[10] but he remained a close friend of the King, admiring him for his geniality and the genuine artistic tastes that he did possess, and he attacked Sir George Mackenzie's somewhat eccentric *Moral Essay, preferring Solitude to Public Employment*. In writing to Cowley he denies to this reply any serious intention, but actually he is anxious to emphasize that even a retired life should be full of useful activity and he gives a brief and conclusive solution of the whole problem in the statement:

> And therefore we are not to measure felicity and repose from the multitude and number of affairs, but from the temper and vertue of the subject; besides that, 'Tis often as criminal to omit doing well as to commit evil, and some wise states have accounted them alike.[11]

9 Houghton, *Collection for the improvement of husbandry and trade*, quoted in Ogg, *England under Charles II*, vol. I, p. 101.
10 *Diary and Correspondence*, ed. Bray, vol. III, p. 138.
11 *Public Employment and an Active Life . . ., Miscellaneous Writings*, ed. Upcott, p. 520.

Evelyn followed this maxim himself, as also did Sir William Temple, who writes in *Upon the Gardens of Epicurus* that:

> . . . the service of the Public is a business of so much Labour and so much Care, that though a good and wise Man may not refuse it, if he be called to it by his Prince or his Country, and thinks he can be of more than vulgar Use, yet he will seldom or never seek it: . . .[12]

Cowley had expected to be called upon by his prince and had been disappointed, but that is not the only reason why, in his Epicurean meditations, he never suggests the possibility of an Epicurean inward calm that would be a source of strength and consolation in all circumstances. For him the life of retirement in the country is an absolute value, and, having accepted the fact that his was a less energetic nature than Temple's or Evelyn's, we may go on to explore the extent of his appreciation of a village community and discuss the virtues that he thinks it encourages.

The urgency to escape from society is pressing:

> If twenty thousand naked *Americans* were not able to resist the assaults of but twenty well-armed *Spaniards*, I see little possibility for one Honest Man to defend himself against twenty thousand Knaves, who are all furnished *Cap a pe*, with the defensive arms of worldly prudence, and the offensive too of craft and malice.

Next to *The Dangers of an Honest man in much Company* is *The Danger of Procrastination*: 'Begin; the Getting out of doors is the greatest part of the Journey.'

Of Myself, though the last essay, provides the best starting-point for a consideration of Cowley's positive values. 'As far as my Memory can return back into my past Life,' he writes, 'before I knew, or was capable of guessing what the world, or glories, or business of it were, the natural affections of my soul gave me a secret bent of aversion from them.' He writes thus at the end of the sequence to emphasize once again that the moods and opinions that have gone before are the basis of his whole character. Even without the supporting evidence of so much of his work, his simple, polite, balanced autobiographical style would be in itself convincing, for example:

> Now though I was here engaged in wayes most contrary to the

12 *Works* (1750), vol. I, p. 171. cf. 'He said . . . he was made for a farmer and not a courtier, and understood being a shepheard and gardener better than an Ambassador'. *Character* by Lady Giffard, *Early Essays*, ed. Moore Smith, p. 29.

> Original design of my life, that is, into much company, and no small business, and into a daily sight of Greatness, both Militant and Triumphant (for that was the state then of the *English* and *French* Courts) yet all this was so far from altering my Opinion, that it only added the confirmation of Reason to that which was before but natural Inclination. I saw plainly all the Paint of that kind of Life, the nearer I came to it; and that Beauty which I did not fall in Love with, when, for ought I knew, it was reall, was not like to bewitch, or intice me, when I saw that it was Adulterate. I met with several great Persons whom I liked very well. . . . I eate at the best Table, and enjoyed the best conveniences for present subsistence that ought to be desired by a man of my condition in banishment and publick distresses; yet I could not abstain from renewing my old School-boys Wish in a Copy of Verses to the same effect.

'All', as Johnson says, 'is easy without feebleness, and familiar without grossness.'

At the end of *Of Liberty* he states the nature of the ideal life to which he wishes to retreat:

> If you ask me in what condition of Life I think the most allow'd [liberty and its attendant benefits]; I should pitch upon that sort of people whom King *James* was wont to call the Happiest of our Nation, the Men placed in the Countrey by their Fortune above an High Constable, and yet beneath the trouble of a Justice of Peace, in a moderate plenty, without any just argument for the desire of increasing it by the care of any relations, and with so much knowledge and love of Piety and Philosophy (that is the study of Gods Laws, and his Creatures) as may afford him matter enough never to be Idle though without Business; or never to be Melancholy though without Sin and Vanity.

His calm assurance that his belief is right and unquestionable enables Cowley to construct an involved enunciatory sentence which is yet completely logical and lucid, the balance of the clauses indicating the harmony and reasonableness of his mind. His slightly challenging opening is toned down into a formal politeness by the colloquial word 'pitch', which yet does not lower it to familiarity. Cowley undoubtedly had a real feeling for this life of 'moderate plenty'. Next to *Of Liberty*, *Of Agriculture* is his longest essay, where, by means of classical conventions and parallels, he gives an admirable account of its value as a way of life and shows himself well aware of its perennial difficulties and problems. He begins with Virgil, the husbandman and philosopher, in the Addisonian sense, and then states the theme of his essay: 'The Utility of it to a mans self. . . . The Innocence, the Pleasure, the Antiquity, the Dignity.' This last he expands at length and laments

> . . . an evil custom, now grown as strong among us, as if it were a Law, which is, that no men put their Children to be bred up Apprentices in Agriculture, as in other Trades, but such as are so poor, that when they come to be men, they have not wherewithall to set up in it, and so can only Farm some small parcel of ground, the Rent of which devours all but the bare Subsistence of the Tenant: Whilst they who are Proprietors of the Land, are either too proud, or, for want of that kind of Education, too ignorant to improve their Estates, though the means to it be as easie and certain in this as in any other track of Commerce: if there were alwaies two or three thousand youths, for seven or eight years bound to this Profession, that they might learn the whole Art of it, and afterwards be enabled to be Masters in it, by a Moderate stock: I cannot doubt but that we should see as many Aldermens Estates made in the Country, as now we do of all kinds of Merchandizing in the City.

Cowley is, however, unduly despondent. The great development in agriculture which took place in the eighteenth century was already beginning. New crops were being introduced and the Georgical Committee of the Royal Society attempted to co-ordinate experiments. Cowley either wrote before this committee was set up in 1664 or was out of touch with its sponsors when he proposed the founding of Colleges of Agriculture in the universities, where the teachers should not be chosen for 'the Ostentation of Critical Literature, but for solid and experimental Knowledge'.[13] His expository prose style is throughout balanced and orderly, occasionally tightening up into the antithetical. Cowley did not wish to be a parasite. He realized as clearly as the greater English Horatians, Ben Jonson and later Pope, that a country community was an organization in which all had duties towards each other and to the whole state, and he attempted, in the face of difficulties, as he tells Sprat, to live the life of a small gentleman farmer;[14] he was 'still in Old England, and not in *Arcadia*, or *La Forrest*'.

13 The subsequent reference to Hartlib is interesting, both because Hartlib was a leading figure in plans of educational reform similar to those advocated by Cowley, here and in *The Proposition*, and because Cowley here ignores or has forgotten that he also published *An Essay for the Advancement of Husbandry-Learning: or propositions for the erecting a College of Husbandry* in 1651. Mr D. Ogg gives an account of Restoration agricultural developments in *England under Charles II*, vol. I, chap. II.

14 Cowley, *Works*, ed. Grosart, vol. I, p. xxvii.

Nevertheless, compared with that of, say, George Herbert, Cowley's conception of country life is decidedly literary. Herbert writes as a spiritual leader who is also a member of the ruling aristocracy, although his scrupulous good breeding and high-minded simplicity allow no trace of arrogance. He had a deep sense of the responsibilities of the gentry as landlords and magistrates and he is interested in all the activities of his flock, even 'old customes, if they be good and harmlesse. . . . If there be an ill in the custome that may be severed from the good, he pares the apple, and gives them the clean to feed on.'[15] That colloquial freshness is very rare in Cowley. Nor does he ever show a taste for anything like Izaak Walton's unsophisticated pastoralism. English rural civilization is the important thing for Herbert and Walton; Cowley's retreat is always implicitly compared to the Sabine Farm; he wishes to be the 'Innocent Deceiver of the World, as *Horace* calls him'.

> When you have pared away all the Vanity what solid and natural contentment does there remain which may not be had with five hundred pounds a year? not so many servants or horses; but a few good ones, which will do all the business as well: not so many choice dishes at every meal, but at several meals, all of them, which makes them both the more healthy, and the more pleasant: not so many rich garments, nor frequent changes, but as warm and as comely, and so frequent change too, as is every jot as good for the Master, though not for the Tailor, or the *Valet de chambre*: not such a stately Palace, nor guilt rooms, or the costliest sorts of Tapestry; but a convenient brick house, with decent Wainscot, and pretty Forest-work hangings. Lastly (for I omit all other particulars, and will end with that which I love most in both conditions) not whole Woods cut in Walks, nor vast Parks, nor Fountains, or Cascade-Gardens, but herb, and flower, and fruit-Gardens which are most useful, and the water every whit as clear and wholesome, as if it darted from the breasts of a marble Nymph, or the Urn of a River-God.

That is the retreat — and most of us could plan something agreeable on, say, £5,000 a year without income tax — described in *Of Greatness* in an interesting modern prose, a more leisurely and less stylized descendant of the Baconian manner. Along with the

15 *Country Parson*, *Poems*, ed. Waller, pp. 285–6. It is interesting that he uses the same metaphor that Cowley uses, in a slightly less concrete way, in my next quotation, but one could not base any conclusions on this difference in usage.

formality goes the characteristic quiet friendliness, showing itself in details of description and in the confiding clause in parentheses in the last sentence. As a horticulturist Cowley is in particular sympathy with Temple and Evelyn. Evelyn, indeed, dedicated to him the second edition of the *Kalendarium Hortense* in 1666 and says that at Chertsey:

> You gather the first roses of the Spring, and apples of Autumn; and as the Philosopher in Seneca desir'd only bread and herbs, to dispute felicity with Jupiter, you vie happiness in a thousand easy and sweet diversions; not forgetting the innocent toils which you cultivate, the leisure and the liberty, the books, the meditations, and above all, the learned and choice friendships that you enjoy, who would not, like you, *cacher sa vie.*[16]

It is, in fact, a social ideal, and 'the conversation of two or three agreeable friends' is an essential part of the scheme; Cowley no doubt remembered the select and brilliant circle that gathered under Lord Falkland's aegis at Great Tew when he was at Oxford in the early years of the Civil War. He now wished to live the life of Augustan decorum and cultivation without the dangerous and disagreeable contacts of the town. Epicurean virtue is both the result of, and the qualification for such a life:

> The first work therefore that a man must do to make himself capable of the good of Solitude, is, the very Eradication of all Lusts, for how is it possible for a Man to enjoy himself while his Affections are tyed to things without Himself? In the second place, he must learn the Art and get the Habit of Thinking; for this too, no less than well speaking, depends on much practice, and Cogitation is the thing which distinguishes the Solitude of a God from a wild Beast. Now because the Soul of Man is not by its own Nature or Observation furnished with sufficient Materials to work upon; it is necessary for it to have continual recourse to Learning and Books, for fresh supplies, so that the solitary Life will grow indigent, and be ready to starve without them; but if once we be thoroughly engaged in the Love of Letters, instead of being wearied with the length of any day, we shall only complain of the shortness of our whole Life.

This passage from *Of Solitude* provides an opportunity to discuss the depth of Cowley's intellectual interests and his claims, if any,

16 *Miscellaneous Writings*, p. 429.

to be called a philosopher. He is here indebted to Montaigne, as indeed is the whole essay, but for us their differences are more interesting than their similarities. Usually their styles point the contrast, Montaigne's rich, vigorous and parenthetical, Cowley's easier, more leisurely and more urbane. Montaigne several times starts him on a train of thought, but he never goes beyond, or even as far as, his predecessor. Whereas Cowley thinks that books are all sufficing, Montaigne writes that:

> Cette occupation des livres est aussi, penible que toute aultre, et autant ennemie de la santé, qui doibt estre principalement considerée: et ne se fault point laisser endormir au plaisir qu'on y prend; c'est ce mesme plaisir qui perd le mesnager, l'avaricieux, le voluptueux, et l'ambitieux. . . . Les livres sont plaisants; mais si de leur frequentation nous en perdons enfin la gayeté et la santé, nos meilleures pieces, quittons les: je suis de ceulx qui pensent leur fruict ne pouvoir contrepoiser cette perte.[17]

The Frenchman's more serious treatment is apparent under the superficial lightness of treatment. This comparison applies all through. Both want to escape from the vices of the world, which however 'nous suyvent jusques dans les cloistres et dans les escholes de philosophies; ny les deserts, ny les rochiers creusez ny la haire, ny les jeusnes, ne nous en desmeslent'[18] because very few are fitted for solitude, and 'if a Mind be possest of any Lust or Passions, a man had better be in a Faire, than in a Wood alone', but where Cowley thinks mainly of occupations for his own leisure in retirement, Montaigne, though no doubt the greater egotist, treats the question in its wider and deeper implications:

> Il fault avoir femmes, enfants, biens et surtout de la santé, qui peult; mais non pas s'y attacher en maniere que nostre heur en depende: il se fault reserver une arriere boutique. . .[19]

Even the cynic must be alone in his own soul sometimes. When Montaigne stresses the value of the simple life in the *Apologie de Raymond Sebond*, it is as part of a penetrating scrutiny of human nature in its universal aspect; Cowley likes the simple life for its own sake. The connection between *Of Greatness* and *De*

17 *Essais*, ed. Le Clerc, vol. I, pp. 213-14. Mr Nethercot has noted Cowley's debts to Montaigne in *Essays of Abraham Cowley, Journal of English and Germanic Philology*, vol. XIXX, pp. 114-30.
18 *ibid.*, p. 207.
19 *ibid.*, p. 209.

l'Incommodité de la Grandeur are equally slight. It is possible that he borrowed the argument beginning:

> The reason of this is, that Greatness has no reallity in Nature, but a Creature of the Fancy, a Notion that consists only in Relation and Comparison . . .

from Montaigne. It is Cowley's most open statement of scepticism. He might, however, equally well have derived it from St. Evremond, the most famous sceptic of the time, whom he knew well, or from any of the French Epicureans, if one must have a source.

Cowley's cult of the retired life represents the extent and seriousness of his Epicureanism. His adhesion to a pagan philosophy amounted to little more than a rationalization of his instinctive tastes. It combined easily with his dilettante interest in Hobbesian materialism and medicine and other branches of science. The conception of the 'mean' as he found it in Virgil, Horace and Martial made a strong emotional impression on him but he ignored its more fundamental implications. He remained like many other English Horatians a devout Anglican. Horace had, of course, been known in England for a very long time; Epicurus's reputation, as distinct from notoriety, dates from the early years of the Restoration. William Charleton published *Epicurus Moralls, collected out of his owne Greek Text in Diogenes Laertius and Partly out of the Rhapsodies of Marcus Antoninus, Plutarch, Cicero and Seneca, and faithfully Englished* in 1656 with a long apologetic introduction. One can imagine how deeply Cowley sympathized with the following accounts of Felicity, the highest good:

> Accordingly, therefore, we affirm; that the Pleasure wherein Felicity doth consist, is only the Former, i.e. in the Stable kind of pleasure: and so can be no other, but the *Indolency of the Body and Tranquillity of the Mind.*

It is not Luxury:

> . . . that can make a Happy Life: But, is Reason, with Sobriety, and consequently a serene Mind; investigating the Causes, why this object is to be Elected, and that to be Rejected; and chasing away the vain, superstitious and deluding opinions, which would occasion very great disquiet in the mind. . . . This Indolent constitution is so far from being a meer Torpor, or sluggishness, as that it is the only state, wherein we can perform all the actions of life vigorously and cheerfully. And, as we

> would not have the life of a wise man to be like a Torrent or rapid river; so would we not have it to be like a standing and dead Pool: but rather as a cleare streame sliding on in a constant silence and gentlenesse.[20]

The remark on the 'Eradication of all Lusts' in the passage already quoted from *Of Solitude* is actually rather Stoic than Epicurean; Epicurus, and his chief seventeenth-century interpreter, Gassendi, taught the moderation of the passions by the rational soul.[21] But Cowley's assertion fits into its context without incongruity because one is not invited by his manner to argue on minute points with him, and in general he tends towards a belief in the supreme Epicurean virtue: that of happiness in a state of quiet and repose, guided by temperance and prudence. Like Metrodorus he thanks 'his own Belly for that moderation in the customary appetites of it, which can only give a Man Liberty and Happiness in this World'. This was the ideal of Guy Patin, François La Mothe Le Vayer and Gassendi who met together at Gabriel Naudé's house at Gentilly where they could escape the violence and licence of life under Anne of Austria's Regency; Cowley may well have known them. In England it was the ideal of Evelyn — in his own way — of Temple and of many others. When Temple writes that the 'wisest and best Part' of mankind 'have chosen what they thought a nearer and surer way to the Ease and Felicity of Life, by endeavouring to subdue or at least to temper their Passions, and reduce their Appetites to what Nature seems only to ask and to need',[22] he relates this amateur Epicureanism to the typical Restoration and Augustan scheme of reason and decorum, the outlook which admired the man 'whose virtue sits easy about him'.[23]

One expects to find in the *Essays* a certain number of references to the new science and ideas suggesting a connection with the Royal Society. There are several, but none of them, excepting the scheme for a school of agriculture, are of particular interest. In *Of Obscurity* we find Cowley saying that:

> . . . I love not *Philosophy* merely notional and conjectural, and no man who has made the Experiment has been so kind as to come back and inform us [about glory after death].

20 *op. cit.*, pp. 22–7 *passim.*
21 See G. S. Brett, *The Philosophy of Gassendi*, chap. II, and F. I. Perrens, *Les Libertins de France, au XVIIème Siècle*, chaps. II and III.
22 *Works* (1750), vol. I, p. 172.
23 *Tatler*, No. 5.

and such phrases as 'knowledge and love of Piety and Philosophy (that is the Study of Gods Laws and of his Creatures)' show that he was conversant with contemporary thought, as he had always been, but by themselves these would not lead one to suppose that he had any great understanding of the implications of Experimental Philosophy. One knows, however, from the ode *To the Royal Society* that he was genuinely interested and deeply impressed.

Sprat, in Part III of his *History of the Royal Society*, emphasizes the value of a leisured country life to progress in scientific studies, and exhorts the nobility to make the best use of their time when they are out of London:

> If they will observe the Generations, Breedings, Deseases, and Cures of *Living Creatures*; their Stables, their Stalls, their Kennels, their Parks, their Ponds, will give them eternal Matter of Inquiry. If they would satisfy their Minds with the advancing of *Fruits*, the beautifying, the ripening, the bettering of *Plants*; their Pastures, their Orchards, their Groves, their Gardens, their Nurseries, will furnish them with perpetual *Contemplations*. They may not only make their *Business*, but their very *Sports* most serviceable to *Experimental Knowledge*. For that, if it be rightly educated, will stand in need of such Recreations as much as the *Gentlemen* themselves, from their hunting, hawking, fishing, and fowling, that is able to receive as much solid Profit, as they Delight.[24]

Possibly a day with Evelyn at Sayes Court inspired this optimism. Cowley made the best of his own property and corresponded with Evelyn on horticultural matters.[25] It is, however, difficult to look upon his *Books of Plants* as evidence of first-hand observation, since Pliny and Fernelius supplied him with much of his matter. In the *Essays* the new science seems responsible for little more than his general tendency to simplify his style,[26] to avoid expressions 'too extravagant and Pindarical for *Prose*'.

* * *

24 *op. cit.*, 2nd ed., p. 406.

25 Letter to Evelyn in Disraeli, *Calamities and Quarrels of Authors*, vol. I, p. 57.

26 The connections between the scientific movement and prose style in the seventeenth century have been described by Mr R. F. Jones in *The Seventeenth Century: Bacon to Pope*. A clarification of prose style similar to Cowley's may be observed by comparing Temple's early writings (*Early Essays and Romances*, ed. Moore Smith) with *An Essay Upon Ancient and Modern Learning* (ed. Spingarn) and Evelyn's translation of La Mothe le Vayer's *Of Liberty and Solitude* (*Miscellaneous Writings*) and the earlier parts of the diary with the later diary, for example, the account of the death of Charles II. The influences of science, of French prose and of journalism were, of course, complex and varying.

Cowley's verse essays continue and partly repeat the thought of the prose, and consequently a certain amount of repetition is inevitable in one's commentary, but at the same time one is able to sum up, just as Cowley's verse gives pointedness and cogency to his prose meditations. It is among his best work.

A comparison of the translations by Cowley and Marvell of Chorus II from Seneca's *Thyestes* provides a starting-point for everything that there is to say about this verse and also clinches my interpretation of the changes in the meaning of wit during Cowley's lifetime.[27] Cowley wrote:

Upon the slippery tops of humane State
    The guilded Pinnacles of Fate,
Let others proudly stand, and for a while
    The giddy danger to beguile,
With Joy, and with disdain look down on all,
    Till their Heads turn, and down they fall.
Me, O ye Gods, on Earth, or else so near
    That I no fall to Earth may fear,
And O ye gods, at a good distance seat
    From the long Ruines of the Great.
Here wrapt in th'Arms of Quiet let me ly;
Quiet, Companion of Obscurity.
Here let my Life, with as much silence slide,
    As Time that measures it does glide.
Nor let the Breath of Infamy or Fame,
From town to town Eccho about my Name.
Nor let my homely Death embroidered be
    With Scutcheon or with Elegie.
    An old *Plebean* let me Dy,
Alas, all then are such as well as I.
    To him, alas, to him, I fear,
The face of Death will terrible appear:
Who in his life flattering his senceless pride
By being known to all the world beside,
Does not himself, when he is Dying know
Nor what he is, nor Whither hee's to go.

Marvell's version runs:

Climb at *Court* for me that will
Tottering favors Pinacle,

27 See chap. I.

All I seek is to lye still.
Settled in some secret Nest
In calm Leisure let me rest;
And far off the publick Stage
Pass away my silent Age.
Thus, when without noise, unknown,
I have liv'd out all my Span,
I shall die, without a groan,
An old honest Country man.
Who expos'd to others Eyes,
Into his own Heart ne'r pry's,
Death to him's a Strange surprise.

I think that Cowley's poem is probably less distinguished than Marvell's but it is the difference in manner, and especially the difference of wit, between the two that concerns me here. One can say little about Marvell's version except that its complete simplicity of diction and delicate subtlety of rhythm manifest a perfect urbanity of tone and an awareness of spiritual issues and profundities which reaches as near as is necessary to explicitness in the final ironic understatement. Marvell's wit is an implicit quality; Cowley's expresses, I think, a somewhat cruder sense 'of other forms of experience which are possible' openly and emphatically. He has less concentration. He starts with six lines of satire which are more solemn and pompous than Marvell's first couplet. He then rises further to the characteristic 'Pindarique' note, which, however, includes a fine image analysed by Hurd: '"long Ruines of the Great" may be taken in two senses, and was probably intended to express them both; namely the oppressive nature of greatness while it stands; and the extensive mischief, that attends its fall'.[28] The next four lines have Cowley's quiet courteous tone and elegiac feeling, and after a more grandiose passage comes the single word which marks most clearly his distance in tone from Marvell; I think that one can localize here one's general sense of the differences between the two poets and that the rest of my account supports what I say about Cowley. The literal translation 'old *Plebean*' shows, I think, the Restoration courtier and scholar in retirement in the country, the Englishman cultivating a classical outlook, the Augustan even, while 'old honest Country man' suggests the Englishman who has

28 *Select Works of Mr A. Cowley*, 3rd ed., vol. II, p. 138.

made the classical tradition his own and who feels the country to be the natural setting of his life, the Jonsonian. Cowley's last six lines introduce a new kind of 'Pindarique' exaggerated note, the Flatmanesque deliberate use of bathos. This implication is the opposite of Marvell's, the insignificance of death suggested underneath the awfulness instead of the awfulness suggested underneath the insignificance. Cowley's method and effect, combining melodrama and the *simpliste*, are cruder. The whole poem clearly derives from the Metaphysical school, but every effect is, as it were, 'spread out' and consequently slightly vulgarized. The poem *Of Solitude*, beginning:

> Hail, *old Patrician Trees*, so great and good!
> Hail ye *Plebeian* under wood!
> Where the Poetique Birds rejoyce,
> And for their quiet Nests and plenteous Food,
> Pay with their grateful voice.
>
> Hail, the poor Muses richest Mannor Seat!
> Ye Country Houses and Retreat,
> Which all the Happy Gods so Love,
> That for you oft they quit their Bright and Great,
> Metropolis above . . .

can be analysed in a similar way, and a comparison of the stanza:

> Thou the faint beams of Reason's scatter'd Light,
> Dost like a Burning-glass unite . . .

with the stanza on the mind in Marvell's *The Garden* brings out very clearly not only differences in the use of imagery between the two poets but also the difference in imaginative power which lies behind. The outstanding quality in Cowley which one is left with is a sense of social decorum modified by his retiring and friendly note, and this is the unifying tone behind the poems discussed in this chapter.

The description and condemnation of what Cowley dislikes occupies rather less space in his verse than in his prose essays. The ode *Upon Liberty* has several interesting stanzas although as a whole it is unsuccessful. The theme is the flight from 'Customs, Business, Crowds, and formal Decency', a revealing list, especially the last. Stanza 2 is based on the account of the patron in the prose essay:

'Tis Morning; well; I fain would yet sleep on;
You cannot now; you must be gone
To Court or to the noisy Hall:
Besides, the Rooms without are crowded all;
The stream of Business does begin,
And a Spring-Tide of Clients is come in.
Ah cruel Guards, that this poor Prisoner keep!
Will they not suffer him to sleep?
Make an Escape; out at the Postern flee,
And get some blessed Hours of Libertie,
With a few Friends, and a few Dishes dine,
And much of Mirth and moderate Wine.
To thy bent Mind some relaxation give,
And steal one day out of thy Life to Live.
Oh happy man (he cries) to whom kind Heaven
Has such a Freedome alwayes given!
Why, mighty Madman, what should hinder thee
From being every day as Free?

The 'Pindarique' loose structure gives Cowley an opportunity to approximate his writing more closely to speech than the couplet allows, and to sketch in a scene by a series of notes. The stanza has the colloquial ease of odes like *Destinie* and *Life and Fame*, but almost completely dispenses with imagery. Presumably this was an effect of the Royal Society's principles which did not, however, operate so much where they more appropriately might have done, namely on his prose. In the group of poems *Of Agriculture*, *The Country Mouse*, a paraphrase of Horace, is a more light-hearted attack on luxury. The City Mouse speaks with amusingly insinuating rhythms:

Let savage Beasts lodg in a Country Den,
You should see Towns, and Manners know, and men:
And taste the generous Lux'ury of the Court,
Where all the Mice of quality resort.

On Avarice he writes a jolly mocking satire, again imitating Horace:

But hold, you whom no Fortune e're endears,
Gentlemen, Malcontents and Mutineers,
Who bounteous *Jove* so often, cruel call,
Behold, *Jove's* now resolv'd to please you all.
Thou Souldier be a Merchant, Merchant, Thou
A souldier be; and Lawyer, to the Plow.

Change all their stations strait, why do you stay?
The Devil a man will change, now when he may,
Were I in General *Jove's* abused case,
By *Jove*, I'de cudgel this rebellious race:
But he's too good: Be all then as you were,
However, make the best of what you are,
And in that state be chearful and rejoyce,
Which either was your Fate, or was your Choice.
No, they must labour yet, and sweat and toil,
And very miserable be a while. . . .

Cowley continually varies the rhythms of his couplets with scraps of direct speech and avoids any approach to solemnity. Most of the verses are less serious on the negative side than the prose. He had not a sufficiently strong poetic talent to write satire of the denunciatory Juvenalian kind except on rare occasions; when satirizing Cromwell in the *Vision* he does so by irony. His verse essays are designed usually, as he says himself, *pour faire bonne bouche* after the prose — a typically Restoration attitude to poetry.

Nevertheless, he hates 'Both the Great, Vulgar, and the small', to use a phrase from *Of Greatness* which became an eighteenth-century commonplace, and in verse as much as in prose he impresses upon us the need to escape from such company.

Begin, be bold, and venture to be wise;
He who defers this work from day to day,
Does on a Rivers Bank expecting stay,
Till the whole stream, which stopt him, should be gon,
That runs, and as it runs, forever will run on.

Johnson draws attention to this as containing 'an example of representative versification which perhaps no other English line can equal'; it shows also better than any comparable lines in the *Davideis* that Cowley was capable of putting his ideas on rhythm into practice.[29]

Cowley expresses his idea of the good life, 'the Prayers and

29 See note 25 to book I of the *Davideis*: 'I am sorry that it is necessary to admonish the most part of readers that it is not by negligence that this verse is so loose, long, and, as it were, vast; it is to paint in the number the nature of the thing which it describes, which I would have observed in divers other places of this poem, that else will pass for very careless verses. . . . The thing is, that the disposition of the words and numbers should be such as that, out of the number and sound of them, the things themselves should be represented.' Cowley's success with these alexandrines varies, but they provided Dryden with a useful model for the winding-up of a paragraph.

Hopes of your Poetick Friend', most solidly at the end of *Of Agriculture*. The translation of Virgil's *O fortunatos nimium* . . . deserves longish quotation:

'Tis True, the first desire which does controul
All the inferiour wheels that move my Soul,
Is, that the Muse me her high Priest would make;
Into her holyest Scenes of Myst'ry take,
And open there to my mind's purged eye
Those wonders that to Sense the Gods deny;
How in the Moon such change of shapes is found:
The Moon, the changing World's eternal bound.
What shakes the solid Earth, what strong disease
Dares trouble the firm Centre's antient ease;
What makes the Sea retreat; and what advance:
Varieties too regular for chance.
What drives the Chariot on of Winters light,
And stops the lazy Waggon of the night.
But if my dull and frozen Blood deny,
To send forth Sp'rits that raise a Soul so high;
In the next place, let Woods and Rivers be
My quiet, though unglorious destiny.
In Life's cool vale let my low Scene be laid;
Cover me Gods, with *Tempe's* thickest shade.
Happy the Man, I grant, thrice happy he
Who can through gross effects their causes see:
Whose courage from the deeps of knowledg springs,
Nor vainly fears inevitable things;
But does his walk of virtue calmly go,
Through all th'allarms of Death and Hell below.
Happy! but next such Conquerors, happy they,
Whose humble Life lies not in fortunes way.

. . . . .

Some with bold Labour plow the faithless main,
Some rougher storms in Princes Courts sustain.
Some swell up their sleight sails with pop'ular fame,
Charm'd with the foolish whistlings of a Name.
Some their vain wealth to Earth again commit;
With endless cares some brooding O're it sit.
Country and Friends are by some Wretches sold,
To lie on *Tyrian* beds and drink in Gold;
No price too high for profit can be shown;

Not Brothers blood, nor hazards of their own.
Around the World in search of it they roam,
It makes ev'n the Antipodes their home;
Mean while the prudent Husbandman is found,
In mutual duties striving with his ground,
And half the year he care of that does take,
That half the year grateful returns does make.
Each fertil moneth does some new gifts present,
And with new work his industry content.
This, the young lamb, that the soft Fleece doth yield,
This, loads with Hay, and that, with Corn the Field:
All sorts of Fruits crown the rich *Autumns* Pride:
And on a swelling Hill's warm stony side,
The powerful Princely Purple of the Vine,
Twice dy'd with the redoubled Sun, does shine. . . .

These are as balanced and vigorous couplets as any Cowley wrote though they lack Drydon's steady onward sweep or Pope's glitter. Pope, nevertheless, remembered and borrowed from the satiric passage.[30] The diction maintains an even decorum, without colloquialisms or excessively Heroic exaggerations. His fancy and judgement are perfectly balanced; as Sir John Denham put it:

Fixt and contemplative their Looks,
Still turning over Nature's Books:
Their Works Chaste, Moral and Divine,
Where Profit and Delight combine;
They guilding Dirt, in noble Verse
Rustick Philosophy rehearse.[31]

The rural scene is 'guilded' and formalized. It is in fact the classical scene, admirably appreciated as it is, but not transmuted into an English scene; Cowley shows no sign of the English interests of the prose essay. Technically he is here close to his contemporary's *Cooper's Hill*, but Denham is closer to the English scene. Allowing for the differences of immediate intention and of the scenes described, it can nevertheless be said that Cowley does not display

30 Or ravish'd with the whistlings of a name (*Essay on Man*, IV.) cf. also:
Sole judge of truth, in endless error hurl'd,
The glory, jest, and riddle of the world!
(*Essay on Man*, II)
with In him he all things with strange order hurl'd;
In him, the *full Abridgement of the World.*
(*Davideis*, I)

31 *On Mr Abraham Cowley. His Death and Burial among the Ancient Poets.*

in these verses any evidence of that profound realization of social responsibilities in country life as it was lived that Pope shows along with his greater polish of style and tone in the *Epistle to Boyle*; Cowley quietly cultivates pleasures that:

> *Horace* might envy in his Sabine Field.

His enthusiasm for his garden is of a more exalted and even more artificial kind. He writes a Pindarique ode in the grand style, in which he ends by comparing himself to an emperor:

> Methinks I see great *Dioclesian* walk
> In the *Salonian* Gardens noble shade,
> Which by his own Imperial hands was made.
> I see him smile (methinks) as he does talk
> With the Ambassadors who come in vain,
>   T'entice him to a throne again.
> If I, my Friends (said he) should to you show
> All the delights, which in these Gardens grow;
> 'Tis likelier much, that you should with me stay
> Than 'tis that you should carry me away:
> And trust me not, my Friends, if every day,
>   I walk not here with more delight,
> Than ever after the most happy fight,
> In Triumph, to the Capital, I rod,
> To thank the gods, and to be thought, myself almost a god.

Using a conversational vocabulary, but developing his thought in long periodic sentences, Cowley achieves a remarkable effect of what M. Loiseau calls oratorical grandeur,[32] so that one feels that he is identifying himself with Diocletian even in the culminating fourteener. Though less sublime, he maintains an elaborate stylization in all his poems on this theme.

The last stanza of the ode *Upon Liberty* brings out by its principal image the bookish character of Cowley's inspiration:

> If Life should a well-order'd Poem be
>   (In which he only hits the White
> Who joyns true Profit with the Best Delight)
> The most Heroique strain let others take,
>   Mine the Pindarique way I'll make.
> The Matter shall be Grave, the Numbers loose and free,

32 *Abraham Cowley: Sa vie: Son œuvre*, bk. II, pt. II, chap. II, I.

It shall not keep one settled pace of Time,
In the same Tune it shall not always Chime,
Nor shall each day just to his Neighbour Rhime,
A thousand Liberties it shall dispense,
And yet shall manage all without offence,
Or to the sweetness of the Sound, or greatness of the Sence. . . .

As an Epicurean he wishes to ſollow his impulses, but reason and prudence are near at hand, and devotion to letters is the chief interest. It was usual to say that poetry had a didactic function, but Neo-Classic critics always began by saying that art imitated life. Cowley's reversal of this idea shows how absorbed he now was in books and literary matters, though the sporting image keeps the gentleman farmer in mind. Cowley seems to have made the impression he desired on contemporaries and successors; Sprat might have had these lines in mind when he wrote the following notes on Cowley's character which serve to round off my account of the *Essays* as his description of their style introduced them:

> . . . He had indeed a perfect natural goodness, which neither the uncertainties of his condition nor the largeness of his wit could pervert. He had a firmness and strength of mind, that was proof against the Art of Poetry itself. Nothing vain or fantastical, nothing flattering or insolent appeared in his humour. He had a great integrity and plainness of Manners, which he preserv'd to the last. . . . He understood the forms of good breeding enough to practise them without burdening himself or others.[33]

And Steele, in recommending prudence and moderation to country gentlemen, invokes the authority of Cowley and commends his magnanimity, which 'is as much above that of other considerable men, as his understanding'.[34]

Cowley's departure from London was a severe shock to the world of letters and Orinda, hearing of it in her remote Welsh hermitage, composed a long ode *Upon Mr Abraham Cowley's Retirement*. Taking the *Essays* as a whole I think that one can say that Cowley achieved the victory that she attributes to him:

Ill-natured world . . .
Thy unwise rigour hath thy empire lost;

33 *Life of Cowley, Critical Essays of the Seventeenth Century*, ed. Spingarn, vol. II, p. 139.
34 *Spectator*, No. 114.

It hath not only set me free,
But it hath made me see,
They only can of thy possession boast,
Who do enjoy thee least, and understand thee most.
For lo, the man whom all mankind admir'd,
(By every Grace adorn'd and every Muse inspir'd)
Is now triumphantly retired.
The mighty *Cowley* this hath done,
And over thee a Parthian conquest won:
Which future ages shall adore,
And which in this subdues thee more
Than either Greek or Roman ever could before.[35]

Cowley, creator of the Pindarique ode, created in his last years another new mode in English writing, the familiar essay. He abandoned the more or less impersonal anthology of *sententiae* for a more varied and more dramatic embodiment of his conclusions about life, in which we feel at every point his presence behind the words and responsibility for what is said. While remaining a serious writer, he writes 'pour amuser les honnêtes gens'. Except for Sir William Temple's *Upon the Gardens of Epicurus* and *Of Health and Long Life*, his essays were unique at the time. Other essays, including Temple's best-known work, had a more public and controversial nature. Addison, Johnson and Goldsmith were his successors.

A NOTE ON COWLEY AND GRAY

Gray's debts to Cowley have not received much attention, perhaps because there is only one reference to him in the *Letters*, since Hurd's edition of the earlier poet.[36] A note upon them will, perhaps, help to clarify Cowley's relation to the Augustans, which has been a theme of this chapter. A certain similarity of tone between the poets is, of course, obvious. Both derived much inspiration from books, and their poetry is full of other men's phrases which came to them naturally and form an integral part of their diction and experience. Gray himself acknowledges two debts to Cowley in his notes to *The Progress of Poesy*, but says nothing about him in connection with the *Elegy*. Bishop Hurd suggests some further borrowings and remarks:

35 Philips, *Poems, Caroline Poets*, Saintsbury, vol. I, p. 576.
36 See also *Notes and Queries*, series I, vol. IV (1851), pp. 204 and 252.

> This excellent writer, not infrequently, alludes to passages in Mr. Cowley, whose manners and genius much resembled his own. Both charm us with the *spleen* of virtue; and both are equally qualified, by gifts of nature, to adorn the nobler and more familiar poetry — The taste, the execution, the success, were happily on the side of our late poet.

I do not find the resemblances, with the exception of:

> *Large was his bounty, and his soul sincere*

and:

> Large was his *Soul* as large a *Soul* as ere
> Submitted to inform a *Body* here,

which has the rhythmic correspondence, as convincing as Hurd did, though they have his endorsement as a personal friend of Gray. There are, however, other key phrases in the *Elegy* which seem to derive from Cowley and to establish his position in the background of the poem.

> Along the cool sequester'd vale of life . . .

is surely developed from:

> In Life's cool vale let my low scene be laid . . .
> (*Of Agriculture*)

and the much admired cancelled stanza:

> Hark! how the sacred Calm, that breathes around,
> Bids every fierce tumultuous passion cease;
> In still small accents whispering from the ground,
> A grateful earnest of eternal peace

seems to associate the vision of Elijah in I Kings 19 with the idealized academic atmosphere of the College of Prophets in the *Davideis*:

> They came, but a new spirit their hearts possest,
> Scatt'ring a sacred calm through every breast . . .
> And thoughts of war, of blood, and murther cease;
> In peaceful times they adore the *God of Peace*. (Bk. I)

These echoes make one wonder whether the line:

> And Melancholy mark'd him for her own

of the later melancholy Cambridge poet represents any kind of sympathetic self-identification with his predecessor who wrote:

> In a deep Vision's intellectual scene,
> Beneath a Bow'r for sorrow made,
> Th'uncomfortable shade,
> Of the black Yew's unlucky green,
> Mixt with the mourning Willow's careful gray,
> Where Reverend *Cham* cuts out his famous way,
> The Melancholy *Cowley* lay . . .

in *The Complaint*, a poem admired by Hurd. The bower and the yew are also part of the setting in the churchyard. At all events Gray seems to have had in the back of his mind not only Milton and Edward King but also Cowley and William Hervey.

This influence of Cowley on Gray, besides illustrating a little further the workings of Gray's imagination, illustrates the continuity and longevity of a poetic tone. Cowley had an important position in the later years of the seventeenth and the early years of the eighteenth centuries as a representative of the Horatian and the elegiac traditions. In surveying English poetry, Pope feels that:

> . . . if he pleases yet,
> His moral pleases, not his pointed wit;
> Forgot his epic, nay Pindaric art,
> But still I love the language of his heart.

Cowley treats melancholy themes with more restraint and decorum than some of his followers who came in for censure from orthodox Augustans. It was Gray's achievement to blend together elements from the Horatian and elegiac strains which Cowley represented with classical pastoral and elegiac elements from Milton into a unity which was 'pensive' and retiring and at the same time reasonable and moderately optimistic, a poem which Augustans could admire. Similarly Cowley's elegy and his essays appealed both to Johnson and to Hurd with his taste for '*sensible reflecting melancholy*'.

6

THE POETRY OF ANDREW MARVELL

THE ATTENTION devoted to Andrew Marvell as a poet during the present century is in conspicuous contrast to the neglect that his work suffered previously. Though the Romantics regarded him as a noble champion of liberty, Coleridge has not even a jotting about his poetry. Marvell is no mere transitional figure — far less so than Cowley — but his work exhibits certain features that are germane to this study. An interpretation of his major poems, made in the light of what has been said about wit and about their literary environment, may therefore help further to illuminate his achievement. 'Illuminate' is, indeed, scarcely an appropriate word, for in reading Marvell one usually finds oneself blinded by excess of light and one's problem is to appreciate the exact configuration of the brilliant surface and to penetrate to the sources of light beyond; Isaac Rosenberg stated the difficulty in his own way when he wrote in a letter, 'Now I think that if Andrew Marvell had broken up his rhythms more he would have been considered a terrific poet'.[1]

Let us first examine the little pastoral, *Clorinda and Damon*, an example of Marvell's lightest manner which nevertheless shows some of the principal features of his genius in an easily observable form — probably this is an early poem,[2] which makes consideration of it now even more appropriate:

1 *Collected Works*, ed. G. Bottomley and D. Harding, p. 317.

2 The chronology of Marvell's poetry cannot be finally settled. I agree with Miss Bradbrook and Miss Lloyd Thomas when they say that *To His Coy Mistress* and *The Definition of Love* are in advance of the other courtly and pastoral poetry and so, presumably, later in date (*Andrew Marvell*, p. 42), but to suggest that there are stylistic reasons for saying that the Fairfax poems might have been written later still (p. 72) seems to me completely erroneous.

C. *Damon*, come drive thy flocks this way.
D. No: 'tis too late they went astray.
C. I have a grassy Scutcheon spy'd,
Where *Flora* blazons all her pride.
The Grass I aim to feast my Sheep:
The Flow'rs I for thy Temples keep.
D. Grass withers; and the Flow'rs too fade.
C. Seize the short Joyes then, ere they vade.
Seest thou that unfrequented Cave?
D. That Den? *C.* Loves Shrine. *D.* But Virtue's Grave.
C. In whose cool bosome we may lye
Safe from the Sun. *D.* not Heaven's Eye.
C. Near this a Fountaines liquid Bell
Tinkles within the concave Shell.
D. Might a Soul bath there and be clean,
Or slake its Drought? *C.* What is't you mean?
D. These once had been enticing things,
Clorinda, Pastures, Caves, and Springs.
C. And what late change? *D.* The other day
Pan met me. *C.* What did great *Pan* say?
D. Words that transcend poor Shepherds skill,
But He ere since my Songs does fill:
And his Name swells my slender Oate.
C. Sweet must *Pan* sound in *Damons* Note.
D. *Clorinda's* voice might make it sweet.
C. Who would not in *Pan's* Praises meet?

Chorus.

Of Pan the flowry Pastures sing,
Caves eccho, and the Fountaines ring.
Sing then while he doth us inspire;
For all the World is our Pan's Quire.

The elegant stylization of this reminds one of Jonson's masques, for example:

Thus, thus begin the early rites
Are due to PAN on these bright nights;
His Morne now riseth, and invites
To sports to dances and delights:
All envious and Prophane away,
This is the Shepherds Holy-day

from *Pan's Anniversary*, and also of *The Rape of the Lock*. 'Scutcheon' might be an Elizabethan decorative image and the repartee has a certain naïvety, but the description of the fountain has a more than Augustan fineness of wit — shells were of course a favourite Palladian and also Baroque motif, while the reference to a soul bathing has both a social and a spiritual connotation, a kind of spiritual good manners, such as one finds in some passages of the earlier Metaphysicals, for example, in Donne's lines to Lady Bedford with their respectful, hesitating movement:

> Therefore I study you first in your Saints,
> Those friends, whom your election glorifies,
> Then in your deeds, accesses, and restraints,
> And what you reade, and what your selfe devize,

and which receive strikingly clear expression in:

> Two Soules move here, and mine (a third) must move
> Faces of admiration and of love,

where one has the impression of the writer's[3] soul going forward to greet those of Donne and Elizabeth Drury as he might have done in the withdrawing-room at Drury House.

The high urbanity of Marvell's conceit is his distinctive contribution to English poetry. It represents a delicate blending of the fine essence of human living, symbolized by the arts of social intercourse, with a sense of the possibilities of achievement in the spiritual life. It is more sophisticated than Herbert and more refined than the Cavaliers. Here the underlying theme of the dialogue, which gives strength to its wit and is in turn strengthened by it, is a simple conflict between the sensual and transitory and the spiritual, and a resolution of that conflict in the conception of Pan or Christ, a traditional identification. Just as Herbert can write an anagram that is none the less a serious poem, so Marvell can argue out a solemn thought in what looks like the lightest of Cavalier conventions.

One can expand this account by discussing a selection of poems representative of the full complexity and depth of his poetry. A few lyrics treat the characteristic seventeenth-century theme of purity,

3 *The Harbinger* to *The Second Anniversary*.
If the poet is Bishop Hall, as is probable, he has of course, besides his personal association with Donne, a place in the history of the heroic couplet. As further illustration of this theme, the following lines from the same poem are an interesting blending of the sacred and the profane, the religious and humanist ideals:

> and let thy Makers praise
> Honor thy Laura, and adorn thy laies.

but the bright precision of the movements has a qualifying and limiting effect. A polite apostrophe sets the intention of the whole of *The Nymph complaining for the Death of her Faun*, including its religious significance:

> The wanton Troopers riding by
> Have shot my Faun, and it will dye,
> Ungentle men!

In *On a Drop of Dew* the idea of the drop whose 'trembling lest it grow impure' is delicately enacted in the rhythm seems to contain an ironic overtone. In contrast to these is the charming *Daphnis and Chloe* which requires a fairly long quotation to bring out its quality:

> I
>
> *Daphnis* must from *Chloe* part:
> Now is come the dismal Hour
> That must all his Hopes devour
> All his Labour, all his Art.
>
> III
>
> But, with this sad News surpriz'd,
> Soon she let that Niceness fall;
> And would gladly yield to all,
> So it had his stay compriz'd.
>
> XXII (Daphnis is speaking)
>
> Gentler times for Love were ment.
> Who for parting pleasures strain
> Gather Roses in the rain,
> Wet themselves and spoil their Sent.
>
> XXIII
>
> Farewell therefore all the fruit
> Which I could from Love receive:
> Joy will not with Sorrow weave,
> Nor will I this Grief pollute.
>
> XXIV
>
> Fate I come, as dark, as sad,
> As thy Malice could desire;
> Yet bring with me all the Fire
> That Love in his Torches had.
>
> XXV
>
> At those words away he broke;
> As who long has praying ly'n,

To his Headsman makes the Sign,
And receives the parting stroke.

XXVI

But hence Virgins all beware.
Last night he with *Phlogis* slept;
This night for *Dorinda* kept;
And but rid to take the Air.

XXVII

Yet he does himself excuse;
Nor indeed without a Cause.
For according to the Lawes,
Why did *Chloe* once refuse?

The first reversal of situation is treated with a crescendo of mock solemnity, the second with gentle irony. Perhaps it is not fantastic to think of Chaucer's attitude to Criseyde; it seems that Marvell was at least familiar with *The Canterbury Tales*.[4] In *Upon Appleton House*, when an elder Fairfax captures his bride from the tutelage of the 'Subtle nuns' of Nunappleton, Marvell treats them with a Hudibrastic jocularity:

Some to the Breach against their Foes
Their *Wooden Saints* in vain oppose.
Another bolder stands at push
With their old *Holy-Water Brush*.
While the disjointed *Abbess* threads
The gingling chain-shot of her *Beads*.
But their lowd'st Cannon were their Lungs;
And sharpest Weapons were their Tongues.

As Marvell never published one cannot prove an influence, but the connection is strengthened by his admiration for Butler's satire when it subsequently appeared.[5] The Marvell is therefore at least an interesting parallel example of the mid-century development of poetic style.[6] His fancy plays lightly with a series of conceits, running swiftly from one to another and getting no more than a burlesque surface effect out of any one of them. It is also one of the rather rare places in Marvell where one can see a matter-of-fact clearly defined use of imagery which leads on to Dryden more obviously than to

4 See *The Rehearsal Transpros'd: Part II*, pp. 169 and 349.
5 *ibid.*, p. 334.
6 cf. *A Dialogue between the Soul and Body* and *The Character of Holland*.

Pope.[7] But Marvell is even here not partisan; he avoids any kind of scurrility or injustice to the Papists; Fairfax

would respect
Religion, but not right neglect.

The satire and the masquelike Metaphysical pastoral both have the same firm human groundwork. Mr Eliot draws attention to how little separates Marvell's outlook from that of the Cavaliers. One has a glimpse of this sympathy in general interests when, for instance, Mrs Hutchinson tells us that her husband bought a number of pictures from the former Royal collection at Whitehall, a gallery which seems to have impressed Marvell, and the fact that Colonel Hutchinson wore his hair long is not entirely irrelevant;

7 Dr F. R. Leavis examines Marvell's relation to the poetry of his century and to the Augustan mode in *Revaluation*, chaps. I and III. There are one or two passages in *Last Instructions to a Painter* where Marvell reminds us of his contemporary, e.g.

Thick was the Morning, and the *House* was thin,
The *Speaker* early, when they all fell in . . .

and the passage about the Secretary, Pett, which have something of Dryden's gusto and humour, but they belonged to different worlds.

Mr van Doren suggests that Dryden may have got the idea for st. 2 of the St. Cecilia Song:

What Passion cannot Music raise and quell?
When *Jubal* struck the chorded Shell . . .
Less than a God they thought there could not dwell
Within the hollow of that Shell . . .

from Marvell's *Music's Empire*:

Jubal first made the wilder notes agree
And *Jubal* tuned Musics *Jubilee*;
He calle'd the *Ecchoes* from their sullen Cell,
And built the Organs City where they dwell.

(*The Poetry of John Dryden*, p. 209.) Looking at Dryden's poem, one wonders whether by chance he got the idea of the pun on chord from Marvell's *Resolv'd Soul and Created Pleasure* (see p. 127).

If Dryden borrowed from Marvell, whom he disliked, in this poem it is interesting that he seems to have shown his admiration for Jonson by borrowing, in the same poem, from *The Musicall strife*; cf.

O sing not you then, lest the best
Of Angels should be driven
To fall againe, at such a feast,
Mistaking earth for Heaven

with

But bright Cecilia rais'd the Wonder high'r:
When to her Organ vocal Breath was given,
An Angel heard, and straight appear'd,
Mistaking Earth for Heaven.

Or is this a mere coincidence due to the common origin? If these plagiarisms are genuine, they show a simple link between two poetic traditions which usually tend to be separate; a manifestation of a common spirit of wit. Dryden transforms the Marvell, but the Jonson already has a declamatory note suggestive of the Restoration — it would probably be straining the evidence to comment further.

Cromwell's interest in music is well known. Marvell's Christian Puritanism differs from, say, Carew's paganism in his more consistent refinement and his deeper seriousness.

In *A Dialogue between the Resolv'd Soul and Created Pleasure* he expounds his principles with a more than Augustan clarity, 'in relation to a wide range of maturely valued interests that are present implicitly in the wit'.[8] In arranging the senses in order of serious allurement he shows his sense of moral proportion, as he shows his feeling for the sensuous beauty of the world in the rhythmic variety of their expression. The simple drama of Christian hero and worldly tempter is Marvell's characteristically precise development of a traditional pattern:

Pleasure.

If thou bee'st with Perfumes pleas'd,
Such as oft the Gods appeas'd,
Thou in fragrant Clouds shalt show
Like another God below.

Soul.

A Soul that knows not to presume
Is Heaven's and its own perfume.

Pleasure.

Everything does seem to vie
Which should first attract thine Eye:
But since none deserve that Grace,
In this Crystal view *thy* Face.

Soul.

When the Creator's skill is priz'd,
The rest is all but Earth disguiz'd.

Pleasure.

Heark how Musick then prepares
For thy stay these charming Aires;
Which the posting Winds recall,
And suspend the Rivers Fall.

Soul.

Had I but any Time to lose,
On this I would it all dispose.
Cease, Tempter, None can chain a Mind,
Whom this sweet Chordage cannot bind.

8 F. R. Leavis, *op. cit.*, p. 28, where there is a detailed analysis of the poem

Each time the soul's replies clamp down on the expansive and resonant phrases of the tempter. The second section is closely bound to the first in the original reading of its opening stanza:

Pleasure.

All this fair, and soft, and sweet,[9]
Which scatteringly doth sine,
Shall within one Beauty meet,
And she be only thine,

and offers more dangerous, because more comprehensive and more clearly defined, temptations, a beautiful woman, enough money to buy the world and power to conquer it, knowledge of 'each hidden cause' and of 'the future time', everything for which successive Faustuses have lost their souls. I have compared Marvell with George Herbert, but whereas Herbert's main theme is the spiritual life and man's relation to God, Marvell sorts out worldly experience in the light of the spiritual and is concerned to compare and evaluate the doings of the human world. The final couplet of *A Dialogue between Soul and Body* sums up a belief in man's original innocence:

So Architects do square and hew
Green Trees that in the Forest grew.

These values form the foundation of Marvell's three most complex Metaphysical poems, *The Definition of Love*, *To his Coy Mistress* and *The Garden*. Here he is not only analysing and comparing but also combining and synthesizing. *The Definition* is a Metaphysical poem in a very strict sense. In it Marvell is engaged in conveying, with incredible ingenuity of imagery and neat formality of rhythms, the idea that perfect love depends on separation in time and space:

II

Magnanimous Despair alone
Could show me so divine a thing,
Where feeble Hope could ne'r have flown,
But vainly flapt its Tinsel wing . . .

9 Mr Margoliouth suggests that this derives from Cowley's
If all things that in *Nature* are
Either soft, or sweet, or fair,
Be not in Thee so *'Epitomiz'd* . . .
(*The Soul*)
It is another of the rather rare places in Marvell where one sees expressed a flicker of feeling shared with his immediate contemporaries — and it is blended at once with Donne (*Aire and Angels*).

V

And therefore her Decrees of Steel
Us as the distant Poles have plac'd,
(Though Loves whole World on us doth wheel)
Not by themselves to be embrac'd.

VI

Unless the giddy Heaven fall,
And Earth some new Convulsion tear;
And, us to joyn, the World should all
Be cramp'd into a *Planisphere.*

The formal argument is reinforced by the relative strength of the images. The chance of a catastrophe annulling the decrees of fate is treated with good-humoured irony in the words 'giddy' and 'cramp'd'. The next stanza carries the situation to a more philosophic plane by a figure from abstract geometry — particularly impressive in the age of Cartesian science:

As Lines so Loves *Oblique* may well
Themselves in every Angle greet:
But ours so truly *Paralel,*
Though infinite can never meet,

which prepares us for the conclusive astronomical pun:

Therefore the Love which us doth bind,
But fate so enviously debars,
Is the Conjunction of the Mind,
And Opposition of the Stars.

Marvell conveys an idea of invisible bonds far stronger than Cowley's public alliance in *Impossibilities*:

As *stars* (not powerful else) when they *conjoin,*
Change, as they please, the World's estate;
So thy *Heart* in *Conjunction* with mine,
Shall our own fortunes regulate,
And to our *Stars themselves* prescribe a *Fate.*

The Definition is restrained and poised in a similar way to the two Dialogues, but *To his Coy Mistress,* while remaining obviously Marvell, has an intensity and richness comparable to Donne's. The rhythms, though no less highly wrought, are much more varied than in any of his other poems, and give a new urgency and seriousness to the traditional theme, 'Vivamus, mea Lesbia, atque amenus . . . ', 'Come, my Celia . . . '. Starting politely, Marvell soon begins his descent to deeper levels of seriousness:

> Thou by the *Indian Ganges* side
> Should'st Rubies find; I by the Tide
> Of *Humber* would complain.

She cares only for useless trinkets, which possibly also suggest drops of his blood, while he waits humbly in the ebb and flow of his grief and love. The chief mood of the stanza is sardonic, showing itself in the mounting exaggeration of:

> I would
> Love you ten years before the Flood:
> And you should if you please refuse
> Till the Conversion of the *Jews*. . . .
> An Age at least to every part,
> And the last Age should show your Heart,

where the irony concentrated in the last line is neutralized by the urbane and businesslike final couplet:

> For Lady you deserve this State,
> Nor would I love at lower rate,

which seems to express a full responsibility for all that has gone before; it is a peculiarly striking example of Mr Eliot's account of wit. In the solemn grandeur of the antithesis:

> But at my back I alwaies hear
> Times winged Charriot hurrying near:
> And yonder all before us lye
> Desarts of vast Eternity,[10]

10 Once again, as Mr Margoliouth notes, Marvell borrows from Cowley, but he reverses the effect of the images:

> On a *Sigh* of Pity I a year can live,
> One *Tear* will keep me twenty at least,
> Fifty a gentle *Look* will give;
> An hundred years on one *kind word* I'll feast:
> A thousand more will added be,
> If you an *Inclination* have for me;
> And all beyond is vast *Eternity*.
> (*My Dyet*)

The tone in which st. 1 ends reminds me rather of Jonson's 'Faire Friend . . . ', e.g.

> I love you at your beauties rate,
> Lesse were an Injurie,

though of course this is a matter of similarity rather than borrowing.

the 'here and now' and the 'there and future' are realized with Marvell's remarkable sense of space and distance.[11] The courtly lyrical note gives an ironic twist to the obituary solemnity in:

> Thy Beauty shall no more be found;
> Nor, in thy marble Vault, shall sound
> My ecchoing Song: then worms shall try
> That long preserv'd Virginity:
> And your quaint Honour turn to dust;
> And into ashes all my Lust,

which reduces both honour and lust to equal insignificance by means of a macabre vision and a whimsically polite evocation of the Anglican Committal. The positive desires latent in the background are brought to light when death is gently burlesqued in the sarcastic comment:

> The Grave's a fine and private place,
> But none I think do there embrace.

One emphatically returns to life in the last stanza, which synthesizes all the varied shades of seriousness and gaiety in the poem:

> Now therefore, while the youthful hue
> Sits on thy skin like morning lew,
> And while thy willing Soul transpires
> At every pore with instant fires,
> Now let us sport us while we may;
> And now like am'rous birds of prey,
> Rather at once our Time devour,
> Than languish in his slow-chapt pow'r.
> Let us roll all our strength, and all
> Our sweetness, up into one Ball:
> And tear our Pleasures with rough strife,
> Thorough the Iron gates of Life.
> Thus, though we cannot make our Sun
> Stand still, yet we will make him run.

The image of the early morning heat haze suggests the extreme

11 cf. Eccho beyond the *Mexique Bay* (*The Bermudas*); or

> How wide they dream! The *Indian* slaves
> That sink for Pearl through Seas profound.
> Would find her Tears yet deeper Waves
> And not of one the bottom sound.
> (*Mourning*)

transience of the moment, and the power of the stanza depends on the contrast between this delicate beauty and the fierce struggle that follows. In the third and fourth couplets 'carpe diem' has become a fight to the death between wild bird and beast. Mr Day Lewis visualizes Marvell and his mistress 'feverishly trying to squeeze an india-rubber ball through the bars of an iron gate',[12] and argues from this that visualization is not part of the required response. Mr Bateson visualizes a simple image of a 'cannon ball crashing through the gates of a town'.[13] Mr Bateson oversimplifies. I think that the cannon ball idea may be somewhere in the background, but Marvell and his mistress are themselves the ball and one is not asked to visualize a feat of contortionism at any stage. As an image, or perhaps one might risk the term symbol, of union the ball is directly evocative, and it has an ancestry in Donne's two hemispheres in *The Good Morrow*. Mr Day Lewis is right in playing down the visual effect of the lines,[14] but the broader sensuous effect, that of muscular effort, is very strong, and increases as we move away from the image of the ball, and the lovers fight themselves free of any hindrances, abstract or concrete, to the full enjoyment of their passion; 'iron gates' is an image of very wide suggestive powers. The increasingly violent imagery and rhythms of these lines work up to, and then come to an abrupt stop in, the project of stopping the sun, 'Time's winged chariot'. Life is conquered, but the victory over time is more apparent than real; one would have to make time move infinitely fast to achieve the same effect as stopping it; Marvell, with blatant false logic, does the best he can.

> . . . yet we will make him run

seems to have triumphant laughter as well as motion in its magnificent rhythm.

Marvell wrote nothing else as concentrated as *To his Coy Mistress. The Garden* deals again partly with the themes of *The Resolv'd Soul and Created Pleasure*, recognition of the value of a rich sensuous life and comparison of the actual to an ideal which is a purification of it. Marvell starts with the idea of retirement and a comparison

12 *The Poetic Image*, p. 72.
13 *English Poetry: A Critical Introduction*, p. 9.
14 It is the vegetable's quality of growth rather than its appearance that is relevant in st. 1. Growth was traditionally the quality in which the vegetable creation excelled all others.

between the limited rewards obtained by most men's nerve-racking activities and the boundless satisfaction to be found in nature:

> How vainly Men themselves amaze
> To win the Palm, the Oke, or Bayes;
> And their incessant Labours see
> Crown'd from some single Herb or Tree,
> Whose short and narrow verged shade
> Does prudently their Toyles upbraid;
> While all Flow'rs and all Trees do close
> To weave the Garlands of repose.

Marvell's conceit fuses the associations of the crowns of military and poetic achievement with a picture of the trees from whose leaves they were made. By equating the inadequate protection these give from the sun with rather prim good advice, he makes an ironical criticism of the achievements for which the crowns used to be bestowed. The rhythmic emphasis on 'all' is very important. The smooth regular movement pauses here as the poem's discovery is first surveyed and stated. It is the rediscovery of Paradise. There follow four further stanzas of exploration in which rhythm and mood change from tentative surprise to assurance and finally rejoicing, from:

> Fair Quiet, have I found thee here
> And Innocence thy Sister dear!

to:

> The *Gods*, that mortal Beauty chase
> Still in a Tree did end their race,
> *Apollo* hunted *Daphne* so,
> Only that she might Laurel grow . . .

and:

> What wond'rous Life is this I lead:
> Ripe Apples drop about my head;
> The Luscious Clusters of the Vine
> Upon my Mouth do crush their Wine;
> The Nectaren, and curious Peach,
> Into my hands themselves do reach;
> Stumbling on Melons, as I pass,
> Insnar'd with Flow'rs, I fall on Grass.

Women are no longer necessary in the Garden, and the Apple and other fruits that suggest the temptations of the flesh can be eaten without any disastrous consequences. At the same time, I think, the very extravagance of the sensuous imagery effects a witty 'placing' of the Garden, which corresponds to the 'placing' of worldly achievements in stanza I. The poet then pauses in his progress and reflects:

> Mean while, the Mind, from Pleasure less,
> Withdraws into its Happiness;
> The Mind, that Ocean where each kind
> Does streight its own resemblance find;
> Yet it creates, transcending these,
> Far other Worlds, and other Seas;
> Annihilating all that's made
> To a green Thought in a green Shade.

Professor Empson once wrote at length on this stanza,[15] and what he says should be carefully considered, though one pulls up short of some of his deeper philosophical interpretations. His interpretation of the first couplet seems odd:

> Either 'from the lessening of pleasure' — 'we are quiet in the country, but our dullness gives a sober and self-knowing happiness, more intellectual than that of the over-stimulated pleasures of the town' or 'made less by pleasure' — 'The pleasures of the country give a repose and intellectual release which make me less intellectual, make my mind less worrying and introspective'.

Is not this a crabbed way of saying 'from the lesser pleasures of public life to those of retirement' and 'from sensual pleasures to intellectual', which form the overt theme of the poem? In any case the Garden is hardly presented as dull. However, having already passed implicit judgement on the outside world and on the sublimated world of the Garden, Marvell makes a further withdrawal, made possible by the special conditions of the 'green shade'. The lines are very complex and have aroused ingenious speculations. Even if one sees little more in them than mystery one can feel the rhythm soar up in triumph and drop in the last line with the calm of fulfilment. I take them to mean that the mind that can reflect the whole visible world and contain a whole world within itself,

15 See '*Marvell's Garden*' in *Some Versions of Pastoral.*

as can the ocean, can also imagine another and yet more satisfying world in which the material world is in fact dissolved into an undifferentiated essence, or quintessence of the principles of natural growth, expressed by 'green', and of thought or reason which are distinctive of mankind. This combines the ideas of destruction for the purpose of re-creation at a higher level, and of annihilation in the seventeenth-century sense of denying the value of, or passing judgement on, the material world.[16] It would seem that Marvell not only contemplates the nature of created things but also understands their worth. He has attained to a godlike wisdom. This interpretation owes something to Professor Empson's [17] but I believe is nearer to what Marvell has written.

After such an achievement the soul's escape from the body comes as something of an anti-climax, serene and contented though it be:

> Here at the Fountains sliding foot,
> Or by some Fruit-trees mossy root,
> Casting the Bodies Vest aside,
> My Soul into the boughs does glide;
> There like a Bird it sits, and sings. . . .

It is one stage from Heaven, but Marvell at once recognizes the impossibility of going even as far as the Garden in a stanza of punning humour of a quite mundane character:

> Such was that happy Garden-state,
> While Man there walk'd without a Mate:
> After a Place so pure, and sweet,
> What other Help could yet be meet!

and ends the poem with a homely maxim:

> How could such sweet and wholesome Hours
> Be reckon'd but with herbs and flow'rs!

16 See note in *Poems of Marvell*, ed. H. M. Margoliouth, p. 226.

17 cf. 'Either "reducing the whole material world to nothing material, i.e. to a green thought", or "considering the material world as of no value compared to a green thought"; either contemplating everything or shutting everything out. This combines the idea of the conscious mind, including everything because understanding it, and that of the unconscious animal nature, including everything because in harmony with it' (*loc. cit.*, p. 119). I feel that at least the last clause is a *non sequitur*, and that the particular philosophic sublety which Professor Empson finds in the poem is his own rather than Marvell's. This is possibly also another of those places where, as Miss Bradbrook and Miss Lloyd Thomas point out (*Andrew Marvell*, pp. 155-6), Marvell's poetry resembles the doctrines of Spinoza.

which after all that has gone before can only be taken wittily. There is a peculiarly fine weighing up and balancing of experiences in this poem.

One could consider *The Mower, Against Gardens* as a kind of comic reply, but as an attack on those who:

> . . . from the Fields the flow'rs and plants allure,
> Where Nature was most plain and pure.

its underlying attitude is similar. This nature where:

> The Gods themselves do with us dwell

has associated with it a correspondingly organic social order of long ancestry. Marvell, as we know, was not a typical Puritan and, later, held a poor opinion of the London of Charles II, but he had deep roots in English life and never seems ill at ease. He is more rooted in English life than Cowley. His 'old honest Countryman' does not claim to be 'an old *Plebean*', and, though one does not find dialect words very often in his verse — 'lew', assuming its authenticity, and 'hewel', a woodpecker, are exceptional — colloquial expressions, such as 'to bird', 'slow-chapt' and the names of flowers, occur in many places.[18] Damon, the idealized mower, cuts the grass of English enclosures and the fauns dance with fairies. For Marvell the country is a place of great natural beauty, filled with both traditional and scholarly associations and also the background of a civilized community. Marvell's urbanity has a more than merely urban connotation. The description of Appleton House:

> Within this sober frame expect
> Work of no foreign Architect. . . .
> And yet what needs there here Excuse,
> Where ev'ry Thing does answer Use?
> Where neatness nothing can condemn,
> Nor Pride invent what to contemn?
>
> A Stately *Frontispiece of Poor*
> Adorns without the open Door;
> Nor less the Rooms within commends
> Daily new *Furniture of Friends*

18 Marvell uses a rich colloquial vocabulary in his prose. The difference between his prose and verse styles is important corroborative evidence of his careful art as a poet.

goes with Jonson's *Penshurst* and Carew's *To Saxham.* It is worth remembering that, besides being the friend of Milton, Marvell was also the friend of Lovelace, the Cavalier *sans peur et sans reproche*, and of John Hales of Eton, the friend of Falkland.

In *An Horatian Ode upon Cromwell's Return from Ireland* the chief character is shown emerging from such a background of unpretentious rural activity:

> And, if we would speak true,
> Much to the Man is due.
> Who, from his private Gardens, where
> He liv'd reserved and austere,
> As if his highest plot
> To plant the Bergamot,
> Could by industrious Valour climbe
> To ruine the great Work of Time,
> And cast the Kingdome old
> Into another Mold.
> Though Justice against Fate complain,
> And plead the antient Rights in vain:
> But those do hold or break
> As Men are strong or weak.

Marvell praises Cromwell in understatements, in which it is difficult not to see irony ('his highest plot') and Charles in urbane drawing-room compliments:

> That thence the *Royal Actor* born
> The *Tragick Scaffold* might adorn:
> While round the armed Bands,
> Did clap their bloody hands.
> *He* nothing common did or mean
> Upon that memorable Scene:
> But with his keener Eye
> The Axes edge did try:
> Nor call'd the *Gods* with vulgar spight
> To vindicate his helpless Right,
> But bow'd his comely Head
> Down as upon a Bed.

The course of events is seen as the product of an ineluctable fate or 'force', which by its heightened expression dominates the human characters in the poem as it did in life, and whose workings are unpredictable; there is also the ghost of a dead king to be laid.

> But thou the Wars and Fortunes Son
> March indefatigably on;
> And for the last effect
> Still keep thy Sword erect:
> Besides the force it has to fright
> The Spirits of the shady Night,
> The same *Arts* that did gain
> A *Pow'r* must it *maintain.*

The italics emphasize his considered and ironical final judgement — if the printed text is any evidence whatever, Marvell seems to have used them sparingly. The poem works by very subtle gradations within its all-embracing mood of urbanity. Mr Eliot describes the humane tradition to which Marvell belongs as essentially that of European and Latin civilization, and when M. Pierre Legouis writes, 'Quant au lecteur français d'aujourd'hui . . . il s'étonnera surtout de se trouver si facilement en communauté d'idées avec le poète pour apprécier la personnalité la plus anglaise qui fut jamais',[19] his aside has more than mere personal value, since it comes as a confirmation from one to whom that tradition is still to some extent the normal intellectual atmosphere. In this poem Marvell set a standard for political verse that has never been surpassed.

Most of his remaining political verse is in decasyllabic couplets, but his place in the history of that form is not important. His two poems on Cromwell are dignified, but only at the beginning of the first and towards the end of the second does one find that fusion of content and technique which makes the words live on the page. Marvell's most distinctive form of couplet writing is a picturesque burlesque, descended from *Upon Appleton House*, for example, the following from *Last Instructions to a Painter*:

> *Ruyter* the while, that had our Ocean curb'd,
> Sail'd now among our Rivers undisturb'd:
> Survey'd their Crystal Streams, and Banks so green,
> And Beauties ere this never naked seen.
> Through the vain sedge the bashful *Nymphs* he ey'd;
> Bosomes, and all that from themselves they hide.
> The Sun much brighter, and the Skies more clear,
> He finds the Air and all things sweeter here.

19 *André Marvell: Poète, Puritain, Patriote*, p. 34.

The sudden change, and such a tempting sight,
Swells his old Veins with fresh Blood, fresh Delight.
Like am'rous Victors he begins to shave,
And his new Face looks in the *English* Wave.
His sporting Navy all about him swim,
And witness their complaisance in their trim.

The blend of sensuous beauty and quietly ironic farce has a remarkable and characteristic freshness, and though the couplets lack polish and flow one thinks of certain passages in Pope:

To happy Convents, bosom'd deep in vines;
Where slumber Abbots purple as their wines:
To isles of fragrance, lily-silver'd vales,
Diffusing langour on the panting gales.[20]

But it was not often that Marvell managed to concentrate all his powers in poetry after 1660. Charles II's government and court seemed to him to threaten all that he believed in as civilization, and he put all his energy into political opposition and religious controversy. In this poem his distress and anger seem to be epitomized in the picture of Charles:

Paint last the King and a dead shade of Night,
Only disperse'd by a weak Tapers light;
And those bright gleams that dart along and glare
From his bright Eyes, yet those too dark with Care.
There, as in the calm horrour all alone,
He wakes and Muses of th'uneasie Throne:
Raise up a sudden Shape with Virgins Face,
Though ill agree her Posture, Hour, and Place:
Naked as born, and her round Arms behind,
With her own Tresses interwove and twin'd:
Her mouth lockt up, a blind before her Eyes,
Yet from beneath the Veil her blushes rise;
And silent tears her secret anguish speak,
Her heart throbs, and for very shame would break.
The Object strange in him no Terrour mov'd:
He wonder'd first, then pity'd, then he lov'd;
And with kind hand does the coy Vision press,
Whose Beauty greater seem'd by her distress;
But soon shrunk back, chill'd with her touch so cold,
And the airy Picture vanish'd from his hold.

20 *Dunciad*, IV, pp. 301-4.

> In his deep thoughts the wonder did increase,
> And he Divin'd 'twas *England* or the *Peace*.

The ironic peripateia validates the elaborate sentimental tragedy, and a total effect is created of single-minded solemnity which looks forward to the mood of another patriotic moralist, Dr Johnson in *London*.

Although one regrets that for the most part he abandoned serious poetry under the Restoration, one is not surprised that Marvell thought it more important to harry the pleasure- and place-seekers who surrounded the Merry Monarch. In any case he had already put on paper a complete poetic vision. He had attained to a political detachment which was above all mere 'faction'; few M.P.s have acquired by the end of their careers the wisdom with which Marvell began his. It required the cruder sensibility of a Dryden to see London as 'the fair Augusta'. Marvell did not retire from it like Cowley, but he shared the feelings of men like Temple and Evelyn who left it on every possible occasion to develop their estates and lay out their gardens. Pope should be considered as his poetic heir — figuratively, as of course there is no evidence of influence. He also could move in a decent social world. Marvell, however, would never have been able to stomach *The Spectator*; like Jonson he belonged to that other England which still had traditions reaching back to Chaucer.

7

THE POETRY OF JOHN NORRIS OF BEMERTON: A PLEA FOR RECOGNITION

THE POEMS of the incumbent of Bemerton in the age of Queen Anne have been undeservedly neglected. He was a not unworthy successor of George Herbert. John Norris, besides occupying an important place on an interesting poetic backwater, is a minor talent of real distinction. He has something to say for which he has discovered an adequate medium, and furthermore he is to be read for whole poems, not merely, as so often with a minor poet, for isolated lines. Norris has not been entirely forgotten; he gets a line or two in histories of literature. But I feel that he needs giving genuine currency, and though I do not claim major status for him, I hope to indicate the sense of 'discovery' one feels after reading through about three-quarters of his volume of pleasing and thoughtful verse on coming upon the poem in which the wheels have indeed taken fire.

At first one is struck by the resemblance to Cowley. *The Retirement* obviously descends from *The Wish*[1] and *The Choice* is a weaker version than Cowley's of Chorus II from Seneca's *Thyestes*; his handful of love poems might have appeared in *The Mistress* — with one exception on which I will comment later. One thinks that here is another belated Metaphysical, using some of the old themes

[1] Cf.
> Well, I have thought on't, and I find,
> This *busie World* is Nonsense all;
> I here despair to please my mind,
> Her sweetest *Honey* is so mixt with *Gall*,

and

> Well then; I now do plainly see,
> This busie world and I shall ne're agree;
> The very *Honey* of all earthly joy
> Does of all meats the soonest cloy. . . .

and devices, but in a new language and with a new tone; at the same time he is obviously not a man of the world, but a scholarly poet writing in retirement.

Besides his borrowings from Cowley, Norris admitted, sixteen years after Dryden had made an example of him in the *Essay of Dramatic Poesy*, to an admiration for Cleveland. In the dedication to *A Murnival of Knaves* (1683), an early work which he did not republish, he expresses the opinion that the Whigs needed 'the pen of a Cleveland, though never so sarcastic, to reduce them to obedience'. It is an ingeniously scurrilous satire of medium quality, the most sustained passage being modelled on *A Hue and Cry after Sir John Presbyter*, for example:

> He can *outgape* bang'd unbrac'd Drums
> With sticks two, fingers eight, two thums,
> Thunder *outnoise* with's deep-mouth'd Bass,
> *Outbray* the Phlegmatick dull Ass;
> With a strange noise laying Hen's *outcackle*,
> Gossips *out-chat* in Prittle-prattle,
> (Whose Musick, if compar'd to thee,
> Is pretty, making Harmonie;)
> *Outgrunt* the Babe of Farrowing Sow,
> *Outlow* little Irish Runt or Cow,
> *Outbellow* too her Consort-Bull,
> *Outscold* the strong-lung'd Drab or Trull,
> *Outbray* in full cry Packs of Dogs,
> *Outcroak* the ugly Toads and Frogs,
> Th'Inhabitants of Fens and Bogs. . . .

Norris's literary ancestry is now clear. He seems to join Butler, Flatman and Mrs Philips as yet another example of how, to the accompaniment of a fitful crackling of squibs, Metaphysical poetry gradually faded out.

His career would fit perfectly into such a pattern. He was born in 1657. Like Flatman, he went to Winchester College. He went on to Exeter College, Oxford, and was later elected a Fellow of All Souls. As an Oxford Platonist he corresponded with Henry More and with Cudworth's daughter, Damaris. He was indeed the last seventeenth-century Platonist and also the only English disciple of Malebranche, his reputation as a philosopher resting on *An Essay towards the Theory of the Ideal and Intelligible Worlds*. Though he greatly admired Descartes, he wrote several works criticizing Locke, who referred to him as 'an obscure enthusiastic man'. He married, and in 1692 he became rector of Bemerton. He kept contact with scholarly circles, especially the 'bluestockings' of the period,[2] and assisted with *The Athenian Mercury*.[3] His *Miscellanies* (1687)[4] ran through five editions in his lifetime. He died in the year of the *Spectator*.

So far however from exemplifying a final senility of the Metaphysical manner, Norris injects a new life into it. In the age of Dryden there were very few poets — Milton, of course, stands apart in every sense — who have any distinction at all. After Dryden himself one descends to Butler and Rochester, the later Cowley and Waller, Traherne, who again does not belong, and Flatman. Norris can compete with any of these lesser men and he can rise above himself as they cannot. Ignored by his contemporaries, as by later readers, he revived for a few years the poetic spirit of the earlier age. Though his poems could only have been written when they were, the Metaphysical element is still a strength, never an incongruity. There is of course a Metaphysical element in the poetry of Pope but it forms part of a larger unity of tone and feeling which is different. In Norris one finds a Metaphysical wit, which, though the emotional and intellectual tension is relaxed, is still

2 See *The Honourable Lovers*: or, the *Second and Last Volume of Pylades and Corinna*, To which is added, *A Collection of Familiar Letters, between Corinna, Mr. Norris. Capt. Hemington, Lady Chudleigh, Lady Pakington, etc.*

3 See *D.N.B.* under Dunton, John.

4 The following is a bibliography of Norris's verse:

(a) *A Murnival of Knaves: or Whiggism displayed* . . . London, 1683.

(b) *Poems and Discourses*, London, 1684. Contents: *Passion of our B. Saviour, Hymn upon the Transfiguration, The Parting, To a Lady, who asked him. What life was, The Third Chapter of Job, Seraphic Love, Atlas Britannicus, Ducis Eboracensis ad Oxonium Processio, The Retirement, The Infidel, On a Musician, The Consolation, The Choice, The Meditation, The Irreconcilable.* With these are included the prose *Of the Care and Improvement of Time, Of Solitude, Of Heroic Piety* and the 2nd ed. of *An Idea of Happiness.*

(c) *A Collection of Miscellanies*: Consisting of *Poems, Essays, Discourses, and Letters, occasionally written*, Oxford, 1687, with *To the Reader*, 1687. Reprint of (b) with important additions; Latin omitted.

(d) 2nd ed. of (c), London, 1692.

(e) 3rd ed. of (c), corrected, London, 1699. *To the Reader* wrongly dated, 1678.

(f) 4th ed. of (c), carefully revised, corrected, and improved by the author, London, 1706. *Advertisement to the Reader* added. Wrong date remains. Revisions of little importance.

(g) 5th ed. of (c), London, 1710. Reprint of (f).

(h) One or two eighteenth-century eds. of *Miscellanies*.

(i) *Miscellanies* in Fuller Worthies' Library, ed. A. Grosart, 1871. Reprint of (g).

(j) *Selected Poems*, J. R. Tutin, Hull, 1905. With Traherne and Henry Vaughan.

recognizably Metaphysical, as the dominant quality of much of his best poetry. As one might expect, he lacks the imaginative poise which enabled even minor poets in the time of Donne and Herbert to control and harmonize such disparate elements in their poetry. His work usually keeps on the serious side of wit, but it includes sometimes a sly humour, which, it is worth noting as a sign of the age he lived in, appears as a decidedly social feature.

Norris seems to have taken some care about the publication of his more reputable poems, and wrote prefaces on his purpose. *To the Reader* of the *Miscellanies* is an interesting document; Norris writes a manifesto stating his conservative attitude to poetry and defying the public:

> Poetry is of late mightily fall'n from the Beauty of its Idea. . . .
>
> 'Tis with this as with our Musick. From Grave, majestic solemn strains, where deep instructive Sense is sweetly convey'd in charming numbers, where equal Address is made to the Judgement and the Imagination, and where Beauty and Strength go hand in hand, 'tis now for the most part dwindled down to light, frothy stuff, consisting either of mad extravagant Rants, or slight Witticisms, and little amorous Conceits, fit only for a Tavern Entertainment . . . and to be a Poet, goes for little more than a *Country Fidler*.
>
> The Design therefore of the present Undertaking, is to restore the declining Genius of Poetry to its Primitive and genuine Greatness, to wind up the Strings of the Muses Lyre, and to shew that Sense and Gracefulness are as consistent in these as in any other Compositions. I design here all the Masculine Sense and Argument of a Dissertation, with the advantage of Poetic Fineness, Beauty and Spirit; and accordingly I have made choice for the most part of Divine and Moral Subject; and if I meddle with any other sort, I commonly turn the Stream another way. . . .

He clearly felt isolated in his epoch and conscious of a change of popular taste and sensibility which he despised,[5] and the fact that he cannot write couplets, as is shown by his pastoral on the death of Charles II, illustrates how little he had in common with his contemporaries; smooth as his lyrics are, his sensibility does not flow with that regular decorum which found the heroic couplet a suitable mould. Period work is represented by his annotated Pindarique

5 In view of the fact that Norris was interested in Cleveland, compare the remarks of the latter's editors (p. 65 above).

odes,[6] and his best, *The Consummation*, is an achievement that improves on Cowley on the same theme and stands comparison with Dryden's vision of judgement at the end of the Killigrew Ode.

'Tis sure th'Arch-angel's Trump I hear,
Nature's great Passing-bell, the *only* Call
Of Gods that will be heard by *all*.
The universe takes the Alarm, the Sea
Trembles at the great Angel's sound,
And roars almost as lowd as he,
Seeks a new Channel, and would fain run under-ground.
The Earth it self does not less quake,
And all throughout, down to the Center shake,
The Graves unclose, and the deep Sleepers there awake.
The Sun's *arrested* in his way,
He dares not forward go,
But wondering stands at the great hurry here below.
The Stars forget their Laws, and like loose Planets stray.

Norris's more characteristic work bears the definite imprint of a personality. *To his Muse* deserves full quotation[7] both for the attitude and the manner of expression:

Come Muse, let's cast up our Accounts, and see
How much you are in Debt to me:
You've reigned thus long the Mistress of my Heart,
You've been the ruling Planet of my Days,
In my spare-hours you've had your part,
Ev'n now my servile Hand your sovereign *Will* obeys.
Too great such service to be Free,
Tell me what I'm to have for being thy Votary.

You have Preferments in your Gift, you say,
You can with Gold my Service pay;
I fear thy Boast, thy sacred Hill I'm told
In a poor, curs'd and barren Country lies;
Besides, what's State to me, or Gold,
These you long since have taught me to despise.

6 cf. the following from the very elaborate explanation of the Platonic *Elevation*: 'In the meanwhile I hope the most rigid maintainer of *Orthodoxy* will allow me the Liberty of alluding to it as an Hypothesis, if not, I'm sure the Laws of *Poetry* will.' With Cowley: 'In fine, whatever the truth be, this opinion makes a better sound in *Poetry*' (*Davideis*, bk. II, note 53), and similar Neo-Classic *loci critici*.
7 As Norris is difficult of access, I quote lavishly throughout this chapter.

To put me off with this, would be
Not to reward, but tax my ill Proficiency.

But Fame you say will make amends for all,
This you your sovereign Blessing call,
The only lasting Good that never dies,
A Good that never can be bought too dear,
Which all the Wise and Virtuous prize,
The *Gods* too with Delight their *Praises* hear.
This shall my Portion be, you say,
You'll crown my Head with an *immortal Bay*.

Give me a place less high, and more secure,
This dangerous Good I can't endure.
The peaceful Banks which profound silence keep
The little Boat securely passes by,
But where with noise the Waters creep
Turns off with Care, for treacherous Rocks are nigh.
Then Muse farewell, I see your store
Can't pay for what is past, and I can Trust no more.

Norris reverses skilfully and with quiet irony the traditional relationship of the poet to his inspirer. He is talking in verse in the language of the coffee-house, but without its coarseness. It is an argumentative lyric without either the close logical structure of the earlier Metaphysicals or the formal reflective manner of the eighteenth century. The image of the boat from Horace[8] gives him a place in a tradition which links the two ages, and if we compare his stanza with Bubb Doddington's borrowing from the same poet:[9]

Void of strong Desires, and Fear,
Life's wide Ocean trust no more;
Strive thy little Bark to steer,
With the tide, but near the shore,

we see that Norris's slightly bantering tone saves him from that air of complacency so often present in eighteenth-century poetry. Norris is not detached and impersonal, but drives his points home by assertion and repetition. He seems on the defensive. One can imagine the isolated and despised philosopher rousing himself and hitting back.

8 *Odes*, II, X.
9 *Odes*, III, XXIX.

Norris writes extremely well on this theme of retirement with his books and friends; there is also a vigorous prose essay, *Of the Care and Improvement of Time*, which exhorts readers not 'to make themselves *Cheap* in the sight of the *Angels*'. He later complained that his parish duties at Bemerton prevented his time from 'being free and entire for [his] own Use and the Service of [his] Friends'.[10] *My Estate* argues further the advantages of his way of life by the successful development of a single figure, ending with a telling and humorous conversational thrust:

How do I pity that proud wealthy Clown
That does with scorn on my low *State* look down!
Thy vain contempt dull *Earth worm* cease,
I wont for Refuge fly to this,
That none of Fortune's Blessings can
Add any *Value* to the *Man*.
This *all* the *wise* acknowledge to be true;
But know I am as *rich, more* rich than you. . . .

Nay (what you'd think less likely to be true)
I can enjoy what's *yours* much more than *you*.
Your Meadow's *Beauty* I survey,
Which you prize only for its *Hay*.
There can I sit beneath a Tree,
And write an *Ode* or *Elegy*.
What to *you care*, does to *me pleasure* bring,
You *own* the *Cage*, I in it *sit* and *sing*.

To Himself, a more ambitious and complex poem on a related theme, is interesting both for its own merit and for its possible topicality:

Not yet Convinc'd? why wilt thou still pursue
Through Nature's Field *delusive* Bliss?
'Tis false, or else too *fugitive* if *true*;
Thou may'st as soon thy *Shadow* overtake as *this*;
The gaudy Light still dances in thy Eye,
Thou hot and eager in the *Chase*
Art drawn through many a thorny rugged Place,
Still labouring and sighing, but can'st ne'er come *nigh*.

Give o'r my Soul, give o'er, nor strive again
This treacherous *Chymic Gold* to find.

10 Letter to Corinna (Elizabeth Thomas) in *Pylades and Corinna*, vol. II, p. 207.

Tell me, why should'st thou *fancy* there remain
Days yet to *come* more sweet, than those thou'st left *behind*.
A wiser Chymist far than thou, t'obtain
    This Jewel all his Treasure spent,
But yet he fail'd in's *grand Experiment*.
And all he gain'd was this, to *know* that *all* was *vain*.

Forbear, and at *another's* Cost be wise,
    Nor longer this *Coy* Mistress *woo*.
He's mad that runs where none can win the Prize,
Why should'st thou lose thy *Mistress*, and thy *Labour* too?
Heaven does but sport with our *Simplicity*
    By laying Jewels in our way,
For when we stoop to seize our *glittering* Prey,
They're snatcht away again, and *baulk* our greedy Eye.

'Tis so, the Choicest good this World can give
    Will never *stand* Fruition's *Test*.
This all by Experience *find*, yet few *believe*,
And in the midst of *Cheats* hope they shall once be *blest*.
Strange *Magic* this. So Witches tho they find
    No Comfort from their *airy* Meat
Forget at next Cabal their *slender* Treat,
And greedily again fall to their *Feast* of *Wind*.

But thou My Soul thy *strong Conviction* shew,
    And never *reach* at *Bliss* again
Our *best* Good here is Nature's *Bounds* to know,
And those Attempt to *spare*, which else would be in *vain*.
Here then Contain thyself, nor higher Good
    In this *inchanted* Place pursue.
And pity those *short-sighted* Souls that do;
This World is best *enjoy'd*, when 'tis best *understood*.

Again Norris is argumentative, and the ordering of the poem through a series of carefully thought-out images to a general summing up is masterly, and poetically convincing; there is an appropriate disillusioned weariness at the start, especially in lines 4 and 8 of the second stanza. The period theme, 'against fruition', is treated in its widest application, though stanza 3 reminds one of another and greater poet, and it seems possible, since this was first published in the *Miscellanies* six years after Marvell's volume, that it is a kind of seventeenth-century poetical reply; the custom of the disputation would have been extremely congenial to Norris by both temperament and training. Marvell would presumably have appeared to him as he did to his future bishop, Burnet, as 'the liveliest droll of the age'; Norris uses the phrase 'vast Eternity' elsewhere,[11] but whether he got it from Marvell or direct from Cowley we can never know. Stanza 2 has some interesting, because oddly and characteristically assorted, period affinities. It suggests the Royal Society as well as the alchemists, and '*Chymic Gold*' may well come from the memorable expression of disillusion with life in Dryden's *Aurengzeb*.[12] In fact, like *To his Muse*, the poem shows Norris's position, in his age but not quite of it. Language and imagery have their connections back, the off-hand tone and the urgent desire to be clear-sighted and to avoid delusions and 'cheats' belong to the time when people were wary of 'the delightful deceits of fables' — witches are comic figures in other Restoration poems — and the theme of restraint, moderation, and the deliberate cultivation of limited objectives looks ahead to the poetical parsons of the eighteenth century.

One may compare *The Complaint*, *Sitting in an Arbour*, *Freedom* and several other poems, and suggest that, if, as Sprat says, Cowley combines in his tone and manner the courtier and the scholar, Norris is the scholar talking to his friends.

> In Native's *Book* were no *Errata's* found . . .

he writes in *A Divine Hymn on the Creation*; 'impertinence' used in its full sense is a key word for what he does not like, and he uses other words, such as 'sympathize' in its primary sense, in a deliberate quasi-technical manner, just as the earlier Metaphysicals use scholastic terminology. Norris himself is also full of scholastic phrases in certain poems and he uses them seriously, whereas Butler, writing at the same time, burlesques the schoolmen. His intellectual values differ considerably from those of the leading figures of his age. He wrote an ode to Dr Plot, the geographer, but as a Christian Platonist

11 *Vide:*
When after some *Delays*, some *dying Strife*,
The Soul stands shivering on the *Ridge* of Life;
With what a *dreadful Curiosity*
Does she *launch* out into the Sea of vast *Eternity!*
(From *The Meditation*, a fine poem.)

12 When I consider life, 'tis all a cheat;
Yet fooled with hope, men favor the deceit. . . .
I'm tired of waiting for this chemic gold,
Which fools us young, and beggars us when old.
(Act IV, Sc. I.)

he seems to have been only very moderately impressed by the scientific discoveries. In *Discouragement* he seeks, while carefully dissociating himself from the sects like any good Neo-Classic, to place the uncertainties of human knowledge in their true perspective:

> This only difference would be
> Between my great *Grandsire*, and me,
> That I my *Paradise* forego
> For want of *Appetite* to know.
>
> 'Tis not that Knowledge I despise;
> No, you misconstrue my Design;
> Or that t'*Enthusiasm* I incline,
> And hope by *Inspiration* to be Wise.
> 'Tis not for this I bid my Books adieu,
> No, I love Learning full as well as you. . . .
>
> . . . for anything I know,
> What we have stamp'd for *Science* here,
> Does only the Appearance of it wear
> And will not pass above, though Current here below;
> Perhaps they've other Rules to reason by,
> And what's Truth here, with them's Absurdity.

A few years before, on the other hand, Cowley in his great *Ode to The Royal Society* had hailed Bacon as the great liberator and re-opener of the Eden of knowledge and thanked the Fellows for showing 'new Scenes of Heaven' and the 'privatest recess' of Nature's 'imperceptible Littleness'. Norris's view is:

> We Truth by a Refracted Ray
> View, like the Sun at Ebb of Day. . . .

The impression of his personality that emerges from the verse is confirmed by a letter from Marissa (Lady Chudleigh) to Corinna, written towards the end of his life:

> He is a little man of a pale complexion, but he has a great deal of sweetness and good humour in his face, attended with an Extraordinary modesty, and more than common air of Humility. There seems to be a reservedness in his temper, but when you're acquainted with him you'll find it only the result of thoughtfulness. In a word, he's a man whose conversation is very agreable as well as Instructive; and as I write to you, one who is very much your friend.[13]

13 *Pylades and Corinna*, vol. II, p. 250.

Norris's distinctively ingenious and amusing love lyric *The Irreconcilable* is, if one bears this account in mind, the more surprising:

> I little thought (my Damon) once, that *you*
> Could prove, and what is more, to *me, untrue.*
> Can I forget such *Treachery*, and *Live?*
> *Mercy* it self would not this Crime forgive.
> *Heaven's* Gates refuse to let *Apostates* in,
> No, that's the *Great unpardonable Sin.* . . .
>
> Go seek *new Conquests*, go you have my Leave,
> You shall not *Grieve* her whom you could *deceive.*
> I don't *lament*, but *pity* what you do,
> Nor take that Love as *lost*, which ne'r was *true.*
> The way that's left you to *befriend* my Fate,
> Is now to prove *more constant* in your *Hate.*

It is a remarkable dramatic achievement in every way. He shows great skill in his control of rhythm and tone. The idiom blends a Restoration formality with certain Cavalier phrases; the poem looks back to the Cavaliers in manners also, but speaks on behalf of Celia (needless to say, 'Orinda' to Norris) — Carew damned *her* for her 'false Apostasy'. Orinda has no more in common with the woman of the new world, the Millamant of:

> Let us be very strange and well bred. Let us be as strange as if we had been married a great while, and as well bred as if we were not married at all,[14]

than Norris himself has with the man of either the old world or the new. He has created a vivid little situation of his own. The series of elegies which may all, as the first does explicitly, commemorate his niece, M.C., are similarly rather nearer to the Cavalier epitaph than to the Augustan. They have a soberly poignant air even when the imagery is of the sort that Johnson was to find blasphemous. *The Grant*, besides showing their ancestry, provides an interesting example of how Norris, like the other late Metaphysical poets, places two attitudes to an experience one after the other instead of fusing them by the power of wit:

> She who her fine-wrought Clay had lately left,
> Of whose sweet *Form* I was bereft,

14 *The Way of the World*, IV, 4.

Was by kind *Fancy* to me brought,
And made the Object of my *happy* thought.
Clad was she all in Virgin white,
And shone with an *Empyrean* Light;
A radiant *Glory* Crown'd her Head,
She stream'd with *Light* and *Love*, and thus she said . . .

What Bliss do we oft to *Delusion* owe!
Who would not still be *cheated* so!

comments the poet at the end in the manner common among poets in the post-Hobbes epoch. We have already noticed his preoccupation with delusions. This time he shows a half-ashamed hankering after them.

Norris's largest and, on the whole, most distinguished group of poems deals with religious themes. Here again certain comparisons must be made and relationships established in order to bring out his qualities as a representative figure and as an individual poetic personality. *Content* shows him in his library, but meditating vaster prospects:

I bless my Stars I envy none,
Not great, nor wealthy, no nor yet the *Wise*,
I've learnt the Art to like my own,
And what I can't attain to, not to prize.
Vast Tracts of Learning I descry
Beyond the Sphere perhaps of my Activity,
And yet I'm ne'er the more concern'd at this,
Than for the Gems that lye in the profound *Abyss*.

It is not the only occasion on which he blesses his stars; the phrase indicates once again the tone of an age.[15] This is devotional poetry written in the dawning age of Reason, Truth and Nature, yet with a trace remaining of an earlier and finer attitude; one notices the mingled pride and hesitancy in 'perhaps'. *The Impatient*, *On Seeing a great Person lying in State*, *Aspiration* and *The Return* all treat this kind of theme with good sense and moderation and a sufficient flexibility of rhythm, but explicit aspiration now usually takes the place of argument. It is significant that Norris nowhere seems to plagiarize or allude to Herbert in his verse, though a letter to

15 cf. Pope's rewriting of Donne's
Sir, though (I thanke my God for it) I do hate . . . (*Satire* II)
as
Yes, thank my stars! as early as I knew . . .

Corinna[16] shows that he rated his predecessor extremely highly. When he attempts in verse a theme that Herbert might have handled he usually fails in the spirit of his time; *Plato's Two Cupids* shows that he cannot blend seriousness and levity in dealing with the central mysteries of Christian belief:

> The Heart of Man's a *living* Butt,
> At which two different Archers shoot,
> Their shafts are *pointed* both with *fire*,
> Both wound our Hearts with *hot desire*. . . .
>
> But he that flames with Love Divine,
> Does not in th'heat *consume*, but *shine*.
> H'enjoys the fire that round him lies,
> Serenely *lives*, serenely *dyes*.
>
> So *Devils* and *damned* Souls in Hell
> *Fry* in the Fire with which they dwell;
> But Angels suffer not the same,
> Altho their *Vehicles* be flame.

This is completely put out of countenance by:

> Love is swift of foot;
> Love's a man of warre,
> And can shoot,
> And can hit from farre.

That note of vulgarity, typical of the Restoration, has here got into Norris's verse, and, oddly enough, shows itself again in other of his religious poems. The Sacred and the Profane have now become separate modes and are best kept apart. Norris did a number of dignified paraphrases of the psalms, and his *Hymn to Darkness* is an admirable solemn invocation. *The Conquest* analyses deeper personal feelings:

> In Power or Wisdom to contend with thee
> Great God, who but a *Lucifer* would dare?

16 *Pylades and Corinna*, vol. II, letter III. He recommends '*The Country Parson's Advice to his Parishioners*, a plain, but very good book, written with great Judgement and Consideration' along with Descartes, Malebranche, Henry More and the Jansenists. Literary connections are rather remote, but it is worth mentioning another characteristic common to the two poets. Walton records Herbert's devotion to music and that he sang on his death-bed. In *A Wish* Norris prays that he may die to the sound of music, and in *The Retractation* he expresses the belief that:

> Only there's *greater* Bliss with Saints above,
> Because they've *better Music* there, and *firmer Love*.

Our Strength is but Infirmity,
And when we this perceive our Sight's most clear:
But yet I will not be excell'd thought I,
In *Love*, in *Love* I'll with my Maker vy.

I view'd the Glories of thy Seat above,
And thought of every Grace and Charm divine,
And further to increase *my* Love
I measured all the Heights and Depths of *thine*.
Thus there broke forth a Strong and Vigorous Flame,
And almost melted down my mortal Frame.

But when thy Bloody Sweat and Death I view
I own (Dear Lord) the Conquest of thy Love,
Thou dost my highest Flights outdo,
I in a lower Orb, and slower move.
Thus in this Strife's a double Weakness shewn,
Thy Love I cannot *equal*, nor yet *bear* my *own*.

The spiritual pride of the first two stanzas is realized in the declamatory and assertive manner. The third, simpler and more concrete in language, subtler in rhythm, especially in the fourth line, and gentler in tone, presents a contrasted mood of humility. Norris learns this more suddenly than Herbert, in *Love*, learns a Christian confidence, but the change of attitude is fully effected in the verse, not merely asserted or pointed to. This poem is an achievement which would be not unworthy of *The Temple*. Norris's mainly argumentative and ruminative poems are often impressive and deserve serious attention, but here he also has the ability to present an experience in the concrete as a clearly defined evolving mood, a far higher poetic quality.

The Passion of the Virgin Mother shows, I think, that Norris was capable of imaginative creation of the supreme kind on a fairly big scale. It is a subject rarely treated by English poets, Anglican or Roman Catholic. He here sinks his own aspirations completely in his theme and achieves the best kind of impersonality. He presents us directly with the closing stages of the drama:

Nigh to the Fatal, and yet Sovereign Wood,
Which crowds of wondring Angels did surround,
Devoutly sad the Holy Mother stood,
And view'd her Son, and sympathiz'd with every Wound.

Angelick Piety in her mournful Face,
Like Rays of Light, through a watry Cloud did shine;
Two mighty Passions in her Breast took place,
And like her Son, sh'appear'd half Human, half Divine.

She saw a blacker and more tragic Scene
Than e'r the Sun before, or then would see;
In vain did Nature draw her dusky Screen,
She saw, and wept, and felt the dreadful Agony.

Grief in the Abstract sure could rise no higher
Than that which this deep Tragedy did move;
She saw in Tortures and in Shame, expire
Her Son, her God, her Worship and her Love.

That sacred Head, which all Divine and Bright,
Struck with deep Awe the Votaries of the East,
To which a Star paid Tributary Light,
Which the (then joyful) Mother kiss'd, ador'd and blest.

That head which Angels with pure Light had crown'd,
Where Wisdom's Seat and Oracle was plac'd;
Whose air Divine threw his Traitors to the Ground,
She sees with pointed Circles of rude Thorns embrac'd.

Those Hands whose Sovereign Touch were wont to heal
All Wounds and Hurts that others did endure,
Did now the Piercings of rough Iron feel,
Nor could the wounded Heart of his Sad Mother Cure.

No, no, it bled to see his Body torn
With Nails, and deck'd with Gems of purple gore,
On four great Wounds to see him rudely born,
Whom oft her Arms a happy burthen found before.

It bled to hear that Voice of Grief and Dread,
Which the Earth's Pillars and Foundations shook;
Which rent the Rocks, and 'woke sleeping Dead,
My God, my God, O why, why hast thou me forsook?

And can the tide of Sorrow rise more high?
Her melting Face stood thick with Tears to view,
Like those of Heaven his setting Glories dye,
As Flowers left by the Sun are charg'd with Evening dew.

He has used the stanza of *Annus Mirabilis* with the last line lengthened to an alexandrine, which he justifies in every case except where he forces a 'Pindarique' repetition upon the Gospel words, to produce a work comparable in strength to, say, Herbert's *The Sacrifice*, but distinctive in language, imagery and tone. The language has the dignified formality and generality of the period — 'Grief in the Abstract . . . ' is probably a tribute from the Platonist in philosophic terms, and in any case represents a minor intrusion by the author into the poem. Yet the poem is no less deeply moving. The linking up of the fifth and sixth stanzas — in sense, despite the punctuation — makes the reader also 'sympathize', to use Norris's term, with the feeling of descent from glory to agony, and the lines in which the pain of the Mother is actually identified with that of the Son through the comparison of his wounds — not the nails — with her supporting arms, have very great imaginative power — intense and complex feeling combined with intellectual ingenuity. This is indeed a Baroque vision, if Baroque implies, as I think it often does, the deliberate turning of suffering to poetic account without losing sight of its harrowing nature. I do not think it particularly likely that Norris borrowed from Crashaw's *Sancta Maria Dolorum*, but an important point about his poem can be made by comparing stanza 8 with:

> O costly intercourse
> Of deaths, and worse,
> Divided loves. While Son and mother
> Discourse alternate wounds to one another;
> Quick Deaths that grow
> And gather, as they come and goe:
> His Nailes write swords in her, which soon her heart
> Payes back, with more than their own smart;
> Her Swords, still growing with his Pain,
> Turn Speares, and straight come home again.

The comparison brings out an interesting exemplification of Norris's ability to make the most of period poetic modes. He has abandoned the simpler language and the physical immediacy of the earlier period along with the ecstatic emotionalism peculiar to Crashaw in favour of a more formal manner, but he has in this particular case achieved a greater strength of phrasing and tautness of rhythm, especially in the powerful contrast of the two lines referred to above. The beautiful last image of my quotation, which places the Mother like a kind of elemental being amid the stricken world of nature, introduces a note of deep poignancy after the violence, and prepares us for the end. The conclusion of the poem is another image of remarkable poetic effect:

> *Gabriel*, the chiefest of th'Almighty's train
> That first with happy Tidings blest her Ear,
> Th'Archangel *Gabriel*, was sent again,
> To stem the tide of Grief, and qualifie her Fear.
>
> A large *Prospective* wrought by hands divine
> He set before her first *enlightened* Eye,
> 'Twas hewn out of the Heaven *Christalline*,
> One of whose ends did *lessen*, th'other *Magnifie*.
>
> With that his Sufferings he expos'd to sight,
> With this his Glories he did represent,
> The weight of this made th'other seem but light,
> She saw the mighty odds, ador'd, and was content.

The extended conceit and pun are superbly effective, both for the mourner in the poem and for the reader, in establishing an attitude of consolation and even detachment. The last line is indeed almost too 'content'; its assurance reminds one a little of the tone of Addison's hymns. But the blemishes are small. One can say, I think, that it is one of those poems in which characteristic elements of two very different styles, the Grand Manner and the style of wit, are fused together into a unity. The poem is completely realized and articulated in every episode of the story. It is a late flowering of Metaphysical wit, but it is clearly related to the masterpieces of the great age. I believe this may be a great poem. One can, I think, safely close one's account of Norris with the impression of it.

Argument about who was the last Metaphysical poet is like argument about who was the last of the Stuarts. If, for a moment, one claims this dignity for Norris, it is fitting in that he had no position in the Augustan world of letters. Nevertheless All Souls and Bemerton were not inappropriate settings for a brief Indian summer of the poetry of piety and of learning.

INDEX